CALLAN
METHOD

Student's Book
Stage 8

English in a quarter of the time!

The Callan ® Method was first developed and published
in 1960 by R.K. T. Callan.

Copyright © Callan Works Limited 2014

First edition by R. K. T. Callan, published for the international market in 2012
This second edition by R. K. T. Callan, published for the international market in 2013

Student's Book – Stage 8
978-1-78229-243-2

CALLAN and the CALLAN logo are registered trade marks of
Callan Works Limited, used under licence by Callan Method Organisation Limited

Printed in the EU

Published by

CALLAN METHOD ORGANISATION LTD.
Ivy Dene, 43 Mill Way, Grantchester, Cambridge, CB3 9ND, UK

www.callan.co.uk

- Para obtener la traducción de este prefacio en español, visitar
  www.callan.co.uk/preface/es

- Per una traduzione di questa prefazione in Italiano, visitare il sito
  www.callan.co.uk/preface/it

- Para obter uma tradução deste prefácio em português, visite
  www.callan.co.uk/preface/pt

- Z polskim tłumaczeniem tego wstępu można zapoznać się na stronie
  www.callan.co.uk/preface/pl

- Pour obtenir la traduction de cette préface en français, rendez-vous sur le site
  www.callan.co.uk/preface/fr

- Bu önsözün Türkçe çevirisi için aşağıdaki web adresini ziyaret edin
  www.callan.co.uk/preface/tr

- 本序言的中文翻译，请访问
  www.callan.co.uk/preface/ch

- 前書きの日本語版の翻訳は次ページをご覧ください
  www.callan.co.uk/preface/jp

- للاطلاع على ترجمة هذه المقدمة باللغة العربية يرجى زيارة •
  www.callan.co.uk/preface/ar

Welcome to the Callan Method

Learning English with the Callan™ Method is fast and effective!

The Callan Method is a teaching method created specifically to improve your English in an intensive atmosphere. The teacher is constantly asking questions, so you are hearing and using the language as much as possible. When you speak in the lesson, the teacher corrects your grammar and pronunciation mistakes, and you learn a lot from this correction.

The Callan Method teaches English vocabulary and grammar in a carefully programmed way, with systematic revision and reinforcement. In the lesson, there is a lot of speaking and listening practice, but there is also reading and writing so that you revise and consolidate what you have learned.

With the Callan Method, the teacher speaks quickly so that you learn to understand English when it is spoken at natural speed. This also means that everyone is concentrating hard all the time.

English in a quarter of the time

The Callan Method can teach English in a quarter of the time taken by any other method on the market. Instead of the usual 350 hours necessary to get the average student to the level of the Cambridge Preliminary English Test (PET), the Callan Method can take as little as 80 hours, and only 160 hours for the Cambridge First Certificate in English (FCE).

The method is suitable for students of all nationalities, and ages. It requires no equipment (not even a whiteboard) or other books, and can be used for classes at private schools, state schools and universities. It is also possible for students to use the books to practise with each other when they are not at school.

In addition to this, students can practise their English online using the interactive exercises, which are available to students who study at licensed schools. Ask your school for details.

The Callan Method in practice

A Callan Method English lesson is probably very different from lessons you have done in the past. You do not sit in silence, doing a reading comprehension test or a grammar exercise from a book. You do not have 'free conversation', where you only use the English you already feel comfortable with. Of course, activities like this can help you, but you can do them at home with a book, or in a coffee bar. In a Callan Method lesson, you are busy with important activities that you cannot do outside the classroom. You are listening to English all the time. You are speaking English a lot, and all your mistakes are corrected. You learn quickly because you are always surrounded by English. There is no silence and no time to get bored or lose your concentration. And it is also fun!

So, what exactly happens in a Callan Method lesson, and how does it work?

The teacher asks you questions

The Callan Method books are full of questions. Each question practises a word, an expression, or a piece of grammar. The teacher is standing, and asks the questions to the students one by one. You never know when the teacher will ask you, so you are always concentrating. When one student finishes answering one question, the teacher immediately starts to ask the next question.

The teacher speaks quickly

The teacher in a Callan Method lesson speaks quickly. This is because, in the real world, it is natural to speak quickly. If you want to understand normal English, you must practise listening to quick natural speech and become able to understand English without first translating into your language. This idea of not translating is at the centre of the Callan Method; this method helps you to start thinking in English.

Also, we do not want you to stop and think a lot about the grammar while you are speaking. We want you to speak as a reflex, instinctively. And do not worry about mistakes. You will, naturally, make a lot of mistakes in the lessons, but Callan Method teachers correct your mistakes, and you learn from the corrections. When you go home, of course it will help if you read your book, think about the grammar, study the vocabulary, and do all the things that language students do at home – but the lessons are times to practise your listening and speaking, with your books closed!

The teacher says every question twice, and helps you with the answer

In the lesson, the teacher speaks quickly, so we say the questions twice. This way, you have another chance to listen if you did not understand everything the first time.

The teacher then immediately says the beginning of the answer. This is to help you (and 'push' you) to start speaking immediately. So, for example:

Teacher: *"Are there two chairs in this room? Are there two chairs in this room? No, there aren't ..."*

Student (immediately): *"No, there aren't two chairs in this room; there are twelve chairs in this room."*

If the teacher does not 'push' you by giving you the beginning of the answer, you might start to think too much, and translate into your language.

The teacher will speak along with you all the time while you are saying your answer. So, if you forget a word or you are not sure what to say, you will always hear the next word or two from the teacher. You should repeat after the teacher, but immediately try again to continue with the answer yourself. You must always try to continue speaking, and only copy the teacher when you cannot continue alone. That way, you will become more confident and learn more quickly. Never simply wait for help from the teacher and then copy – you will not improve so quickly.

Long answers, with the same grammar as the question

We want you to practise your speaking as much as possible, so you always make complete sentences when you speak in the lesson, using the same grammatical structure as in the question. For example:

Teacher: *"About how many pages are there in this book?"*

Student: *"There are about two hundred pages in that book."*

In this way, you are not just answering a question; you are making full sentences with the vocabulary and the grammar that you need to learn.

Correction by imitation

With the Callan Method, the teacher corrects all your mistakes the moment you make them. The teacher corrects you by imitating (copying) your mistake and then saying the correct pronunciation/form of the word. For example, if you say "He come from Spain", the teacher quickly says "not come - *comes*". This correction by imitation helps you to hear the difference between your mistake and the proper English form. You should immediately repeat the correct word and continue with your sentence. You learn a lot from this correction of your mistakes, and constant correction results in fast progress.

Contracted forms

In the lesson, the teacher uses contractions (e.g. the teacher says "I don't" instead of "I do not"). This is because it is natural to use contractions in spoken English and you must learn to understand them. Also, if you want to sound natural when you speak, you must learn to use contractions.

Lesson structure

Every school is different, but a typical 50-minute Callan lesson will contain about 35 minutes of speaking, a 10-minute period for reading, and a 5-minute dictation. The reading practice and the dictation are often in the middle of the lesson.

In the reading part, you read and speak while the teacher helps you and corrects your mistakes. In the dictation, you practise your writing, but you are also listening to the teacher. So, a 50-minute Callan lesson is 50 minutes of spoken English with no silence!

No chatting

Although the Callan Method emphasises the importance of speaking practice, this does not mean chatting (free conversation). You learn English quickly with the Callan Method partly because the lessons are organised, efficient, fast and busy. There is no time wasted on chatting; this can be done before or after the lesson.

Chatting is not a good way to spend your time in an English lesson. First, only some of the students speak. Second, in a chat, people only use the English that they already know. Third, it is difficult for a teacher to correct mistakes during a conversation.

The Callan Method has none of these problems. All through the lesson, every student is listening and speaking, practising different vocabulary and structures, and learning from the correction of their mistakes. And nobody has time to get bored!

Repeat, repeat, repeat!

Systematic revision

In your native language, you sometimes read or hear a word that you do not already know. You usually need to read or hear this new word only once or twice in order to remember it and then use it yourself. However, when you are learning a foreign language, things are very different. You need to hear, see and use words and grammatical structures many times before you really know them properly. So your studies must involve a system of revision (repeating what you have studied before). This is absolutely essential. If there is no system of revision in your studies, you will forget what you have studied and will not be able to speak or understand better than before.

In every Callan Method lesson, of course you learn new English, practise it, and progress through your book. However, you also do a lot of revision so that you can really learn what you have studied. Your teacher can decide how much revision your class needs, but it will always be an important part of your studies.

Also, because there is a lot of revision, it is not important for you to understand everything the first time; it gets easier. The revision with Callan is automatic and systematic. Every day you do a lot of revision and then learn some new English.

Revision in reading and dictation too

The reading and dictation practice in the lessons is part of Callan's systematic revision as well. First, you learn a new word in the speaking part of the lesson; a few lessons later, you meet it again when you are reading; finally, the word appears in a dictation. This is all written into the Callan Method; it happens automatically.

Correcting your dictations

With the Callan Method, there is little or no homework to do, but it is very important that you correct your dictations. These are printed in your book and so you can easily correct them at home, on the bus, or wherever. It is important to do this because it helps you to learn the written forms of the words you have already studied in earlier lessons.

Your first lessons with the Callan Method

During your first lesson with the Callan Method, all of the questions and some of the vocabulary are new for you; you have not done any revision yet. For this reason, the teacher may not ask you many questions. You can sit and listen, and become more familiar with the method - the speed, the questions, the correction etc.

History of the Callan Method – Robin Callan

 Robin Callan, who passed away in April 2014, was the creator of the Callan Method. In addition to owning the Callan School in London's Oxford Street, he also ran Callan Method Organisation Ltd. This company, now managed by a dedicated team of Callan Method professionals, continues to grow, supplying Callan Method books to schools all over the world.

Robin Callan grew up in Ely, Cambridgeshire, England. In his early twenties, he went to Italy to teach English in Salerno. Although he enjoyed teaching, Robin thought that the way in which teachers were expected to teach their lessons was inefficient and boring. He became very interested in the mechanisms of language learning, and was sure that he could radically improve the way English was taught.

He remained in Italy and started to write his own books for teaching English. He used these in his own classes and, over the following ten years, gained an immense amount of practical experience and a reputation for teaching English quickly and effectively.

When he returned to England, he opened his school in Oxford Street. As the Method became more and more popular with students, the school grew and moved to larger premises. Robin continued to write his Callan Method books, and today the Method is used by schools all over the world.

Robin Callan was always passionate about English literature, especially poetry. For this reason, he bought The Orchard Tea Garden in Grantchester, near Cambridge, which attracts thousands of tourists each year. Throughout the 20th century, it was a popular meeting place for many famous Cambridge University students and important figures from English literature, such as Rupert Brooke, Virginia Woolf and E.M. Forster. Today, it is also home to the Rupert Brooke Museum.

Mr Callan lived in Grantchester for many years, and played an active role in the management of his companies well into his retirement and old age. He left an amazing legacy on which we all continue to build.

The Callan School in London's Oxford Street

The largest private school in London

The Callan School in Oxford Street is the largest private school in London teaching English as a foreign language. Depending on the time of year, the school employs between 60 and 100 teachers and has an average of 1600 students passing through its doors every day. This number rises to more than 2000 in the middle of summer, similar to a small university.

Websites

Please visit the following websites for more information:

Callan Method http://www.callan.co.uk

Lots of information, including a list of schools around the world that use the method

Callan School London http://www.callanschoollondon.com

All you need to know about the largest private English language school in London

How Callan Method Stages compare to CEFR* levels and University of Cambridge General English exams

* Common European Framework of Reference

It is difficult to compare the Callan Method books directly with the CEFR levels and Cambridge exams, but below is an approximate guide.

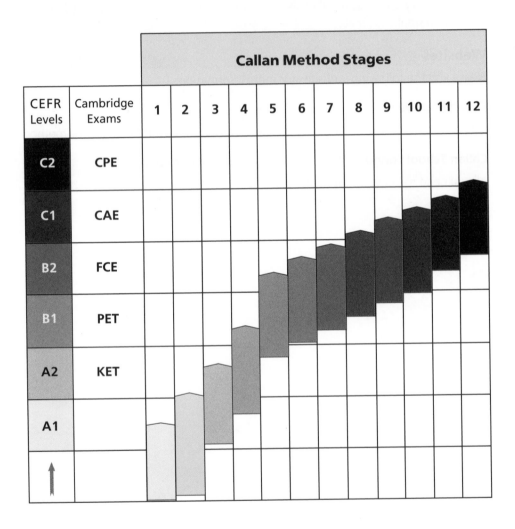

CEFR Levels	Cambridge Exams	Callan Method Stages											
		1	2	3	4	5	6	7	8	9	10	11	12
C2	CPE												
C1	CAE												
B2	FCE												
B1	PET												
A2	KET												
A1													
↑													

STAGE 8

STAGE 8

603 **joke**

Do you like people who are always laughing and joking?   Yes, I like ...
                                                                ~ No, I don't like ...

Can you tell us a joke?   Yes, I can tell you a joke
                                                                ~ No, I can't tell you a joke

pretend

What am I pretending to do?   You're pretending to play
                                                                the piano, kick a football etc.

When children play together, do they often pretend to be adults?
                                                                Yes, when children play ...

If you see someone you know in the street but you're in too much of
a hurry to stop and say hello, do you sometimes pretend not to notice
them?   Yes, if I see ..., I sometimes pretend ...
                                                ~ No, if I see ..., I never pretend ...

envelope   stamp   leave out   postcode

What do we have to put on an envelope before posting a letter?
                                                We have to put an address and a stamp on ...

If you write the address on the envelope but leave out the postcode, will
the letter still arrive?   Yes, if you write ..., the letter
                                                will still arrive, but it may take longer

604 What am I pretending to do?   You're pretending to stamp
                                                a piece of paper with a stamp

naturally

Would you find it difficult to behave naturally if you met someone really
famous?   Yes, I'd find it ...
                                                                ~ No, I wouldn't find it ...

What do I mean if I say "Naturally, she was pleased about passing the test"?

> If you say "Naturally, she ...", you mean "Of course, she ..."

recent   so-so

What is the most recent film you have seen?

> The most recent ...

What was it like – that is, was it good, bad, or just so-so?

> It was ...

Have you been to any concerts recently?

> Yes, I've been ...
> ~ No, I haven't been ...

mate   housemate   flatmate

classmate   workmate

What can we say instead of the word "friend" in very informal English?

> We can say "mate" instead of ...

What's a housemate or flatmate?

> A housemate or flatmate is someone who we live with

Do you know the names of all your classmates?

> Yes, I know ...
> ~ No, I don't know ...

605 If you thought one of your workmates was stealing money from the company you worked for, what would you do?

> If I thought one of ..., I'd ...

to look forward to

If you are looking forward to something, it means that you are waiting for it with pleasure. For example, "I always look forward to going on holiday".

Is there anything you're really looking forward to doing at the moment?

> Yes, there's something ...
> ~ No, there isn't anything ...

What?

What kind of things do you look forward to most?

> The kind of things I ... are ...

let me see

The expression "Let me see" means "Give me time to think for a minute".

What does the expression "Let me see" mean?
The expression ...
"Give me time to think for a minute"

On what kind of occasions do we use it?
We use it on
occasions when we are
thinking about something and
we are not completely sure of the answer

606   chance   dismiss   jungle

fifty-fifty   take a chance

If you were the owner of a business and one of your workers stole something from the business, would you give them a second chance, or would you dismiss them at once?
If I were ... from
the business, I'd ...

Why?

Supposing there was a place, shall we say, somewhere in the middle of a jungle in South America, where you knew for sure that there was about fifty million pounds' worth of gold, but the chances of returning alive were only fifty-fifty, would you go and take a chance and try your luck, or would you just stay at home and dream about it?
Supposing there was ...
where I knew ... only fifty-fifty, I'd ...

Why?

whistle

What am I doing?
You're whistling

hunt

Many years ago, did humans have to hunt animals for food?
Yes, many years ago, humans ...

607 deed

Why should we judge a person by his deeds more than by his words?

> We should judge ... because it's
> easier to say things than to do them

grease

What do we use grease for?

> We use ... to make the
> different parts of a machine move smoothly

scissors

What do we use a pair of scissors for?

> We use a pair of
> scissors for cutting paper etc.

take control   **lose control**

If you were in a bus going downhill and the driver suddenly lost control of the bus, what'd you do?

> If I were ...,
> I'd try to take control of the bus etc.

due   **due to**

What might happen if you didn't pay your electricity bill when it was due?

> If I didn't pay ..., they might
> come and cut the electricity off ...

When are you due to come here again?

> I'm due to ...

Why don't trains always arrive when they are due?

> Trains don't ...
> because of bad weather, breakdowns etc.

608 When a person is rich, do you think it's due to the fact that they're more intelligent than most other people, or do you think it's mainly due to luck?

> When a person ..., I think it's ...

grandmother   **grandfather**

great-grandmother   **great-grandfather**

Were your grandmothers both born in the same country as you?

Yes, my grandmothers were both ...
~ No, my grandmothers weren't both ...

What do we call our grandfather's father?

We call ...
our great-grandfather

mostly

Are the people in this country mostly tea drinkers or coffee drinkers?

The people in ... are mostly ...

Do you think that passing exams is mostly a question of luck?

Yes, I think ... ~ No, I don't think ...

totally

Do you think your language is totally different from English?

Yes, I think ... ~ No, I don't think ...

If a friend of yours is wearing clothes that look totally wrong on them, do you tell them?

Yes, if a friend ..., I tell them
~ No, if a friend ..., I don't tell them

609 **Idiom 13**

let yourself go = relax and enjoy yourself

e.g. The party was a great success; everyone really let themselves go.

What does the idiom "let yourself go" mean?

The idiom ...
"relax ..."

Give me an example, please.

If you relax a little and
let yourself go, you'll feel happier

 *Dictation 74*

The court was deadly silent/ as the judge sentenced the criminal/ to life in prison./ The man was not/ very badly hurt in the accident,/ which happened on the station platform,/ but he was taken to hospital/ to see the doctor,/ just to be on the safe side./ It is irritating that/ he always confuses/ the meaning of the words/ "rough" and "smooth"./ When judging anything,/ we should always try to look/ under/ the surface of things/ and see things as they really are.

 Do Revision Exercise 49

LESSON 113

610   **discuss**   **discussion**   **argue**   **argument**

       quarrel   **anger**   **reason**

If people discuss something with each other, it means that they talk about something in a serious or formal manner. People often express different opinions in a discussion but it is rarely unpleasant.

If people argue about something with each other, it means that they disagree strongly on a subject and become angry.

If people quarrel about something with each other, it means that they lose control of their anger, and start shouting and saying unpleasant things to each other.

Therefore, we could say that two people could begin by quietly discussing a subject, the discussion could then develop into an argument, and the argument could finish in a quarrel.

What's the difference between "to discuss", "to argue" and "to quarrel"?
> The difference ... is that
> "to discuss" means to talk about ...,
> "to argue" means to disagree badly ...,
> and "to quarrel" means to lose control ...

Do you enjoy discussing politics?
> Yes, I enjoy ...
> ~ No, I don't enjoy ...

Why do housemates sometimes argue with one another?
> Housemates sometimes ... because ...

Did you quarrel a lot with your brother or sister when you were a child?
> Yes, I quarrelled a lot with ...
> ~ No, I didn't quarrel a lot with ...

611 **Another meaning of the verb "to argue" is "to reason". For example, "He argues that he could not finish the job because he didn't have sufficient time", or "His argument for not finishing the job was that he didn't have sufficient time".**

Give me an example of the word "argue" used with the meaning of "to reason".

> She argues that if we don't go now it'll be too late

regular   **do something about**

What does it mean "to live a regular life"?

> "To live a regular life" means that we eat, sleep and work etc. at more or less the same times every day

Would you say that a regular life was better than an irregular one?

> Yes, I'd say ... ~ No, I wouldn't say ...

Why or why not?

Can a dentist do anything about irregular teeth?

> Yes, a dentist can ...

Do you work (or study) irregular hours?

> Yes, I ... ~ No, I don't ...

blow up

Why is it important to blow up bridges during a war?

> It's important to blow up ... in order to make it difficult for the enemy to get across the river; to do so, they would either have to swim, cross by boat or build new bridges

612 **dust**   **powder**   **collect**

face powder   **meeting**   **football match**

Red Cross

The difference between "dust" and "powder" is that dust is natural and collects on objects. For example, if a table is not cleaned for a long time, you will find dust on it. Powder, on the other hand, is something that is made. For example, washing powder is powder we put into a washing machine to clean our clothes, and face powder is powder made for the face.

What's the difference between "dust" and "powder"?   The difference
between dust and powder is
that "dust" is natural and collects on
objects, whereas "powder" is something that is made

Have you ever collected stamps or anything like that?   Yes, I've
collected ... ~ No, I've never collected ...

On what kind of occasions do people collect together in large numbers?
The kind of occasions on which
people collect together in large numbers are
parties, political meetings, football matches etc.

Do they collect money in the streets in your country for different causes,
such as for the Red Cross, the poor etc.?   Yes, they collect ...
~ No, they don't collect ...

What do you consider to be a good cause worth collecting money for?
I consider ... to be a ...

613 **furniture**   **furnish**

What kind of furniture do you like to see a room furnished with?
I like to see a room furnished with ...

available

How long does it usually take for a new film to become available to buy?
It usually takes ...

If you rang somebody up when they were at work but they weren't
available immediately, would you wait, leave a message or call back later?
If I rang ..., I'd ...

human being

Do you think that human beings sometimes behave worse than animals?
Yes, I think ... ~ No, I don't think ...

artificial

What artificial parts of the body can science provide us with?
Science can provide us with
artificial arms, legs, teeth, hair etc.

Plural of nouns and third person singular of verbs

kiss	rush	hero

Generally speaking, when a word ends in the letters "o", "s", "x", "z", "ch" or "sh", we form its plural, if it is a noun, and its third person singular of the present simple tense, if it is a verb, by adding the letters "es" to it. For example, "one potato – two potato<u>es</u>" and "I go – you go – he go<u>es</u>". The word "piano" is an exception; we say "one piano – two pianos".

When do we add the letters "es" to form the plural of a noun and the third person singular of a verb?
> We add the letters … when a word ends in the letters "o", "s", "x", "z", "ch" or "sh"

Give me some examples, please – both noun and verb.
> "one potato – two potatoes"; "I go – you go – he goes"

If the noun or verb ends in a consonant plus "y", the "y" is changed to "i" and then the letters "es" are added. For example, "one lady – two lad<u>ies</u>" and "I cry – you cry – he cr<u>ies</u>".

What happens when a noun or verb ends in a consonant plus "y"?
> When a noun or verb …, the "y" is changed to "i" and then the letters "es" are added

Give me an example, please – both noun and verb.
> "one lady – two ladies"; "I cry – you cry – he cries"

If you kiss your mother hello, how many kisses do you give her – one, two or three?
> If I kiss …, I give her … kisses

What do we mean by the rush hour in a large city?
> By the rush hour …, we mean the time when everyone rushes to work or home from work

Who were your heroes when you were a child?
> My heroes when I … were …

Why?

Idiom 14

pull someone's leg = joke with someone, by making them believe something that is not true

e.g. All right, don't get angry. He was only pulling your leg.

What does the idiom "pull someone's leg" mean?

The idiom ... "joke with someone ..."

Give me an example, please.

After all these years of knowing him, I still don't know when he's being serious and when he's just pulling my leg

 *Dictation 75*

The man was charged with committing/ one of the most serious crimes/ that anyone can commit,/ and it was totally clear/ right from the beginning/ that he was guilty./ If you invited me to your house,/ I'd be your guest,/ and you'd be my host./ People are not usually good/ at drawing straight lines/ without the help of a ruler./ One of the best things for a headache/ is to lie down and relax.

LESSON 114

dish   **serve**

The difference between a plate and a dish is that a plate is flat, whereas a dish is deeper. We usually eat food from a plate, whereas we serve food from a dish. The word "dish" can also mean food made in a particular way, such as fish and chips or chilli con carne.

What's the difference between a dish and a plate?   The difference between ... is that ...

What's your favourite dish?   My favourite dish is ...

Do you know how to make it?   Yes, I know ...
        ~ No, I don't know ...

to be for (or against) something

arms   fox   fox hunting

Are you for or against the police carrying arms when they're walking around the streets on duty?   I'm for ... ~ I'm against ...

Why?

Are you for or against fox hunting?   I'm for ... ~ I'm against ...

Why?

seize   **handbag**

What do members of the general public do when they see a criminal seize a woman's handbag in the street?   When members of the general public see ..., some run after the criminal or shout for help, but most people just stand and look too surprised to do anything

break out

What would you do if another world war broke out? If another world war broke out, I'd ...

wage   **salary**   **payment**

profession   **non-professional**

We use the words "wage" and "salary" for the payment received for work done. The difference between "wage" and "salary" is that we generally use the word "wage" for a non-professional job, or a job in which a person earns a fixed amount of money for each hour they work, whereas we generally use "salary" for a professional job, or a job in which a person earns a fixed amount of money each year.

What's the difference between "wage" and "salary"? The difference between ... is that ...

steady   **seasonal**   **seaside**

painter   **pianist**   **surgeon**

What kind of people don't earn a steady wage or salary? The kind of people who ... are actors, artists, writers etc.

618 Do seasonal workers, such as waiters who work at seaside hotels in the summer, receive a wage or a salary? Seasonal workers ... a wage

What kind of jobs do we need a steady hand for? The kind of jobs we need a steady hand for are painter, surgeon, pianist etc.

About how long do you think it'll take you to finish this book if you keep working steadily? I think it'll take me about ... to finish ...

Plural of nouns ending in "f" or "fe"

leaf   **loaf**   **shelf**   **cliff**

When a noun ends in "f" or "fe", we generally make its plural by changing the "f" or "fe" to "ves". For example, "leaf – leaves", "loaf – loaves", "shelf – shelves", "knife – knives", "life – lives", "wife – wives" etc. However, three common exceptions to this rule are "chefs", "cliffs", and "roofs".

How do we generally form the plural of a noun ending in "f" or "fe"?

> We generally ... by changing the "f" or "fe" to "ves"

Give me some examples, please.

> leaf – leaves ...

What are three common exceptions to this rule?

> Three common exceptions to ... are "chefs", "cliffs" and "roofs"

deer   **wood**

What's the plural of "deer"?

> The plural of "deer" is "deer"

Where do deer prefer to live: in woods or open fields?

> Deer prefer to live in woods

Why?

> Because they are usually afraid of human beings and other animals

619 **mention**

What kind of things do people often mention when they're telling you about a holiday they've just been on?

> People often mention the weather, the food etc. when ...

Give me another sentence with the word "mention" in it, please.

> In his speech to his employees, he mentioned that there was a possibility of wages being increased

tell off

When does a mother tell off her child?

> A mother ... when the child has done something wrong and made her angry

partner

If you went into business, would you prefer to have a partner or to be alone?   If I went into ..., I'd prefer ...

Why?

insist

If a friend buys you a drink in a bar, do you normally insist on giving them the money or do you just buy them a drink the next time?
                                                                            If a friend buys ..., I ...

620   **board   floorboard   noticeboard   blackboard**

deck   port   director

The basic meaning of the word "board" is a flat piece of wood. From it, we get "floorboard", "noticeboard", "blackboard" etc.

What's the basic meaning of the word "board"?   The basic ... a flat
                                                                  piece of wood

Give me some examples of what we get from the word "board".
                                                  Some examples of what ... are
                                              "floorboard", "noticeboard" etc.

What do we use a noticeboard for?   We use a noticeboard for putting
                                              notices on. It is a quick and easy way
                                          of giving news and information to everybody

From the idea that the deck of a boat is made from wooden boards, we get the verb "to board" and the expression "on board". We use these when we are talking about getting on or being on boats, ships and planes.

Do you have to show your passport before you can board a plane?
                                                              Yes, I have to ...

What would happen if you went on board ship to say goodbye to a friend and you remained on board after the ship had left port?   If I went ...,
                                      I'd have to leave the ship at the next available port

We can also use the word "board" with the idea of a table, and from this we get, for example, "a board of directors", which is a group of directors who control a company or other organization. As these people usually meet round a table, we call their meeting a "board meeting".

What do we mean by a "board of directors"?   By a ...
                                                                    we mean a group ...

621 What do we mean by a "board meeting"?   By a ...
                                                          we mean a meeting of
                                              company directors round a table

Also from the idea of a table, we use "board" with the idea of the food we are given when we stay at a hotel. If we pay for "full board", we get breakfast, lunch and dinner. If we pay for "half board", we get breakfast and dinner only. Alternatively, we can simply pay for "bed and breakfast".

If you stayed at a hotel on holiday, would you choose "full board", "half board" or "bed and breakfast"?   If I stayed ...,
                                                                    I'd choose ...

Idiom 15

see eye to eye = agree with someone

e.g. Richard and his wife see eye to eye on most things.

What does the idiom "see eye to eye" mean?   The idiom ...
                                                          "agree with someone"

Give me an example, please.   She doesn't see eye to eye
                                with her parents about the plans for the wedding

 *Do Revision Exercise 50*

LESSON 115

Present simple for the future

timetable   **schedule**

We use the present simple to speak about a future action when we are talking about timetables or schedules. For example, we can say "The film starts at 10 p.m.", "My train leaves in fifteen minutes", or "England play football against Germany next Saturday".

Give me an example of the present simple for the future, please.

The meeting starts at 3 p.m. tomorrow

When does this lesson finish?

This lesson finishes at ...

Do you know when your local football team play their next game?

Yes, I know when my ...
~ No, I don't know when my ...

account

Give us a short account of what you did yesterday.

Yesterday, I ...

Give us a short account of the last film you saw.

The last film I saw
was ...; it was about ...

Do you have a bank account?

Yes, I have ...
~ No, I don't have ...

Do you have an account at any shop?

Yes, I have ...
~ No, I don't have ...

623 Do you keep an account of all the money you spend?

Yes, I keep ...
~ No, I don't keep ...

Why or why not?

greedy   **satisfied**   **crop**

Are greedy people ever satisfied with what they have?

No, greedy
people ...; they always want more

Why is a farmer never satisfied with the weather?   A farmer is never satisfied ... because, whatever the weather is like, it's never perfect for every type of crop that he's growing

differ

Do your eyes differ in colour from mine?   Yes, my eyes differ ...
~ No, my eyes don't differ ...

What sometimes happens if two people differ greatly in their opinions on a particular subject?   If two people differ greatly ..., they sometimes have an argument

private

Have you ever had private English lessons?   Yes, I've had ...
~ No, I've never had ...

Is it impolite to ask questions about someone's private life unless you know them very well?   Yes, it's impolite to ...

624   Relative clauses (3)

We have already learned a lot about relative clauses, but here are a few more things that we should know.

what

We use the relative pronoun "what" instead of "which" or "that" when we don't mention the thing that the relative clause describes. For example, instead of saying "She showed me <u>the dress which</u> she had bought", we can say "She showed me <u>what</u> she had bought".

When do we use the relative pronoun "what"?   We use ... when we don't mention the thing that the relative clause describes

Give me an example, please.   She told the waiter what she wanted

When you were a child, did you always like what you were given for your birthday?

> Yes, when I was ..., I always ...
> ~ No, when I was ..., I didn't always ...

Have you already chosen what you're going to eat this evening?

> Yes, I've already chosen what I'm ...
> ~ No, I haven't chosen what I'm ... yet

whom

With formal English, some people prefer to use the relative pronoun "whom" instead of "who". However, this is only possible when the relative pronoun is not the subject of the verb that follows.

In the sentence "I recognized the criminal who stole the bag", the word "who" is the subject of the verb "stole"; in this sentence, we cannot use "whom".

625　However, in the sentence "I recognized the criminal <u>who</u> the policeman arrested", the word "who" is not the subject of the verb "arrested"; "the policeman" is the subject and "who" is the object. In this case, some people prefer to use the word "whom" instead of "who" and say "I recognized the criminal <u>whom</u> the policeman arrested". In informal English, however, the word "whom" is never used.

When do some people prefer to use the relative pronoun "whom" instead of "who"?

> Some people ... with formal English, when the relative pronoun is not the subject of the verb that follows

Give me an example, please.

> The gentleman whom he informed was the manager

If you were employed by someone whom you disliked, what would you do?

> If I ... whom I disliked, I'd ...

In very formal English, we sometimes have a preposition at the beginning of a relative clause, and in this case we cannot follow the preposition with the word "who"; we <u>must</u> use "whom" instead. For example, "She is the lady <u>with whom</u> I had a conversation", or "The manager <u>to whom</u> I sent the document has not replied". (Remember, however, that in normal spoken English we put the preposition at the end, and say "She's the lady <u>who</u> I had a conversation <u>with</u>", or "The manager <u>who</u> I sent the document <u>to</u> hasn't replied".)

When we have a preposition at the beginning of a relative clause, can we follow the preposition with the word "who"?   No, when we have …, we cannot follow the preposition with "who"; we must use "whom"

Give me an example, please.   We need to contact the customer from whom she took the payment

Do you know the nationality of all the students with whom you are studying at the moment?   Yes, I know … ~ No, I don't know …

626 In normal spoken English, what do we say instead of "We need to contact the customer from whom she took the payment"?   In normal spoken English, instead of …, we say "We need to contact the customer who she took the payment from"

whose

We use the word "whose" at the beginning of a relative clause instead of using a possessive adjective like "my", "your", "his" etc. For example, instead of saying "I have a dog. Its tail is long", we can say "I have a dog whose tail is long". Instead of saying "Yesterday I visited Mr Jones. I work with his sister", we can say "Yesterday I visited Mr Jones, whose sister I work with".

When do we use the word "whose" at the beginning of a relative clause?   We use the word "whose" … instead of using a possessive adjective like "my", "your", "his" etc.

Give me an example, please.   The woman whose handbag was stolen is on her way to the police station

Do you know the people whose house is next to yours?   Yes, I know … ~ No, I don't know …

search

Why do the police use dogs when they are searching for a criminal?   The police use dogs when … because dogs have an excellent sense of smell

Have you ever been searched at an airport?   Yes, I've been … ~ No, I've never been …

support

What supports this ceiling?　　　　　　　　　　The walls support ...

627　Do you support any particular football team?　　　　Yes, I support ...
　　　　　　　　　　　　　　　　　　　　　　~ No, I don't support ...

Idiom 16

watch your step = be careful

e.g. You'll have to watch your step or you'll find yourself in great difficulty.

What does the idiom "watch your step" mean?　　　The idiom ...
　　　　　　　　　　　　　　　　　　　　　　　"be careful"

Give me an example, please.　　　　　　　　You have to watch your
　　　　　　　　　　　　　　　step when you do business
　　　　　　　with people you know nothing about

religious

 *Dictation 76*

Forgetting that/ the doorway was low,/ I received a severe blow/ on my head/ as I went through it./ Children are taught/ that they should respect their elders./ He lived in a period/ when people were burned alive/ for their political and religious opinions./ They had no children of their own,/ so they adopted one./ A person who is not a born leader/ can, nevertheless,/ sometimes be taught leadership./ That particular king is considered/ one of the cruellest figures/ in English history.

LESSON 116

628 **declare**   **red-handed**   **innocent**

If you were caught red-handed stealing something, would you declare yourself innocent before the judge when you appeared in court for your trial?
Yes, if I were ..., I'd ...
~ No, if I were ..., I wouldn't ...

Why or why not?

When was the last time your country declared war on another country?
The last time my ... was ...

Do you think it's always wise to declare your future plans to other people?
Yes, I think it's ... ~ No, I don't think it's ...

Why or why not?

upper	**middle**	**working**
class	**society**	**aristocracy**
industrialist	**case**	**lower**

We sometimes refer to people in society as being "upper class", "middle class" or "working class". If we say that someone is upper class, we mean that they are very rich or have a lot of power in society. The upper class are often members of the aristocracy, or are powerful industrialists. By "middle class", we mean people who are not particularly rich or poor. They are usually professional people such as lawyers, doctors, teachers etc. By "working class", we mean people who have the least power and money in society. They often do physical work. The idea of "class" in society differs from country to country, but "upper", "middle" and "working" are the basic divisions.

629   What do we call the three classes into which many societies in the world are divided?

> We call the three ... the upper class, middle class and working class

What do we mean when we say that someone is upper class?

> When we say ..., we mean that they are very rich or have a lot of power in society

When describing written English, by "upper case" letters and "lower case" letters we mean "capital" letters and "small" letters.

In writing, what do we mean by upper case and lower case letters?

> In writing, by ... we mean capital letters and small letters

Is this the upper part of my head?

> No, that isn't the ...; it's the lower ...

How is it sometimes possible for a shop to make more profit if it lowers the prices of its goods?

> It's sometimes ... because a lot more people decide to buy its goods

raise	to be excused	monument	honour

statue

What's another word we can use instead of "lift"?

> Another word ... "raise"

What does it generally mean when a pupil raises their hand in the air during a lesson?

> When a pupil ..., it generally means they want to ask a question, or to be excused; that is, to be given permission to leave the room

630   Which do you think are more expensive to raise: children or racehorses?

> I think ... are more ...

Why?

If you were a great person, what kind of monument would you like the public to raise in your honour after you were dead?

> If I were a ..., the kind of monument I'd like ... would be a statue etc.

The difference between a transitive verb and an intransitive verb is that a transitive verb has an object, whereas an intransitive verb does not have an object.

The verb "to raise" is transitive; that is, it has an object. For example, "I (subject) am raising (verb) the book (object)".

The verb "to rise", however, is intransitive, which means that it does not have an object. For example, "The book (subject) is rising (verb)".

What's the difference between a transitive verb and an intransitive verb?
> The difference ... is that a transitive verb has an object, whereas an intransitive verb does not have an object

What's the difference between the verbs "to raise" and "to rise"?
> The difference ... is that "to raise" is transitive, whereas "to rise" is intransitive

Give me some sentences containing transitive verbs, please.
> The car hit the wall. The boy cut his thumb. They pushed the table. He opened the door.

631 Right, now give me some sentences containing intransitive verbs, please.
> The sun rises at 6 o'clock. He gets up very early in the morning. People walk very quickly in winter. The door opened.

Note that the object of a transitive verb is not always stated. For example, in the sentence "He ate quickly", the object of the verb is obviously the food that he ate, although this is not stated.

Is the object of a transitive verb always stated?   No, the object of ...

Give me an example, please.   He ate quickly

respect   scorn   worthy

Do you think it's more important for managers to have the respect of employees or to be liked by employees?   I think it's ...

What is scorn?

Scorn is a feeling that somebody or something is not worthy of our respect

term

Which school term are children in at the moment?

Children are in the ... term at the moment

worship

Where do people go to worship?

People go to worship in a church, mosque, synagogue, temple etc.

632 **cattle**   **cowboy**

How does a cowboy keep his cattle together?

A cowboy ... together by constantly riding around them on a horse or motorbike

harvest

What happens at harvest time?

Farmers gather their crops ...

mother-in-law   **father-in-law**

When a man is married, what does he call his wife's mother and father?

When a man is married, he calls ... his mother-in-law and father-in-law

What's a brother-in-law?

A brother-in-law is the brother of our wife or husband, or the husband of our brother or sister

What's the plural of "brother-in-law"?

The plural ... is "brothers-in-law"

rail   railing   run   protection   balcony

A rail is a piece of metal or wood which is long and thin. For example, a train runs on rails, which is why we call it a railway train.

What's a rail?

A rail is a piece of ...

Why do we call a train a railway train?	We call a train a railway train because it runs on rails

633 **Railings are several pieces of metal or wood which we put around things for protection. We find railings on a balcony to stop people falling, or sometimes around a piece of private land to stop people entering.**

What are railings?	Railings are several pieces ...
Where do we find railings?	We find railings ... balcony ... piece of private land ...

Idiom 17

to be on about = to mean

e.g. What's he on about? I can't understand what he's trying to say.

What's the meaning of the idiom "to be on about"?	The meaning ... "to mean"
Give me an example, please.	I tried to explain what the problem was but I don't think he understood what I was on about

 *Dictation 77*

It was a very serious matter,/ which grew out of nothing,/ and was totally unexpected./ The poor dog/ caught its tail in the door/ and hurt itself./ The president had been elected/ twice previously./ A trade union is an organization/ which protects the workers./ Most butchers, bakers/ and workers in other trades/ belong to unions./ It was extremely difficult,/ but they finally managed/ to rescue the sailor from the island.

 *Do Revision Exercise 51*

LESSON 117

634 **Words not used in the plural**

knowledge   **progress**   **item**   **encyclopedia**

Some English nouns are never used in the plural. For example, the words "advice", "furniture", "information", "knowledge", "progress" and "news" do not have plural forms. We don't say "All those informations were useful"; we say "All that information was useful". However, we can sometimes communicate a plural idea with nouns like this by using expressions such as "pieces of" or "items of". For example, we can say "All those pieces of information were useful" or "I need to buy five new items of furniture".

Name some English nouns that are never used in the plural, please.

> Some English nouns ... are "advice", "furniture", "information", "knowledge", "progress" and "news"

Which of these sentences is correct: "He hasn't made many progresses" or "He hasn't made much progress"?

> "He hasn't made much progress" is correct

How can we sometimes communicate a plural idea with nouns like this?

> We can sometimes ... by using expressions such as "pieces of" or "items of"

Give me an example, please.

> She gave him two pieces of valuable advice

Do you agree that a little knowledge can sometimes be a dangerous thing?

> Yes, I agree that ...
> ~ No, I don't agree that ...

Why or why not?

> Because we might get completely the wrong idea about something if we only know half the facts ~ Because knowing a little about something is better than knowing nothing

635 What do you think is the best piece of advice a father can give to his son?

> I think the best ... is ...

Why?

Does an encyclopedia contain pieces of information about all kinds of subjects?   Yes, an encyclopedia contains pieces of ...

mass	advantage	disadvantage
mass-production		production
product	identical	quality

Do you think that the masses should be educated to the age of eighteen?
                                        Yes, I think ... ~ No, I don't think ...

Why or why not?

What would you say were the advantages of mass-production?
                                        I'd say the advantages of
                                        mass-production were that products
                                        can be made quickly and more cheaply

And what would you say were the disadvantages?   I'd say ... the
                                        products are often identical,
                                        and the quality might sometimes be poor

pick up	date	vocabulary

What am I doing?   You're picking your pen up from the floor

636 When a boy and a girl have a date, is it more common for the boy to pick the girl up at her house or to meet her somewhere in town?
                                        When a boy and a ...,
                                        it's more common for ...

Do you sometimes pick up new English vocabulary from songs?
                                        Yes, I sometimes ... ~ No, I never ...

prevent

What do you think is the best way to prevent accidents on the roads?
                                        I think the best way ...

drum

What am I doing?   You're drumming your fingers on the table

What's the difference between a drum and a barrel?

The difference between ... is that a drum
is usually made of metal and has straight sides,
whereas a barrel is usually made of wood and has round sides

What would you do if your next-door neighbour played the drums loudly every evening?   If my ..., I'd ...

harbour   port

Although the words "harbour" and "port" are similar in meaning, a harbour is anywhere a boat or ship is protected from the weather, whereas a port is a place where goods are put onto or taken off a ship, or where passengers board a ship. We also use "port" to mean a town or city with a port. For example, Liverpool is a port.

What's the difference between the words "harbour" and "port"?

The difference ... is that a harbour ...

637 nosey

What do we mean if we say that someone is nosey?   If we say ...,
we mean that they are too
interested in other people's private matters

Have you got nosey neighbours?   Yes, I've got ...
~ No, I haven't got ...

Nouns with different forms

masculine   feminine

In English, there are a few nouns that are different depending on whether we are talking about a man or a woman. We call these nouns "masculine" if they refer to a man and "feminine" if they refer to a woman.

We can sometimes form a feminine noun from a masculine noun by adding the letters "ess".

actor	–	actress	waiter	–	waitress
host	–	hostess	god	–	goddess
prince	–	princess			

How can we sometimes form a feminine noun from a masculine noun?

> We can sometimes form ... by adding the letters "ess"

638 What are the feminine forms of "actor", "host" etc.?

> The feminine forms of ... are "actress", "hostess", "princess", "waitress" and "goddess"

Other examples of masculine and feminine nouns are as follows:

nephew	–	niece
landlord	–	landlady
widower	–	widow

What are the feminine forms of "nephew", "landlord" and "widower"?

> The feminine forms of ... are "niece", "landlady" and "widow"

event	eventful	uneventful

What has been the most important event of your life so far?

> The most ... so far has been ...

Why?

What type of sports event do you like to watch most?

> I like to watch ... most

Would you say you had led an eventful or uneventful life?

> I'd say I'd led ...

concern

Are you the kind of person who likes to put his nose into things that don't concern him?

> Yes, I'm the kind of ...
> ~ No, I'm not the kind of ...

celebrate   **celebration**   **New Year's Eve**

If you won the lottery, how would you celebrate?   If I ...,
                                                              I'd celebrate by ...

Do most countries have a big celebration on New Year's Eve?   Yes,
                                                                  most ...

up to date   **out of date**   **essential**

Do you always buy clothes that are up to date?   Yes, I always ...
                                                    ~ No, I don't always ...

If you're planning to travel around the world, is it essential to have an up-
to-date passport?   Yes, if you're planning ...,
                                                      it's essential ...

If you bought some food in a supermarket and then discovered it was out
of date, would you take it back?   Yes, if I ..., I'd ...
                                                    ~ No, if I ..., I wouldn't ...

Idiom 18

a piece of cake = extremely easy to do

e.g. This town is full of hotels, so finding somewhere to stay will be a piece of
cake.

What does the idiom "a piece of cake" mean?   The idiom ...
                                                    "extremely easy to do"

Give me an example, please.   Most of the questions
                                        in the exam were really difficult,
                                but the first three were a piece of cake

LESSON 118

···

640 **<u>Using nouns in the general sense</u>** **article**

In the sentence "Dogs hate cats", we are not speaking about specific dogs or cats. We mean dogs generally and cats generally.

When we use nouns in the general sense, we put them in the plural and we do not put an article ("a", "an" or "the") in front of them. For example, "<u>Schools</u> educate <u>children</u>" or "<u>Machines</u> help <u>people</u> do <u>jobs</u>". If a noun does not have a plural form, we simply use it on its own, also without an article. For example, "<u>Bread</u> is commonly eaten with <u>butter</u>" or "<u>Blood</u> is red".

When we use nouns in the general sense, what do we do with them?
When we ..., we put them in the plural
and we do not put an article in front of them

Give me an example, please.
People go to cinemas to watch films

What do we do if a noun doesn't have a plural form?
If a noun ..., we simply use it on its own, also without an article

Give me an example, please.
Paper comes from wood

Is it correct to say "The water is necessary for the life"?
No, it isn't ...

What must we say instead?
We must say "Water is necessary for life" instead

641 **<u>Definite article</u>** **<u>Indefinite article</u>**

The articles in English are "the", "a" and "an". We call the word "the" the definite article, and we call the words "a" and "an" the indefinite articles. We use "a" before a word that starts with a consonant sound, whereas we use "an" before a word that starts with a vowel sound.

What are the articles in English?

The articles in English are "the", "a" and "an"

What do we call the word "the"?

We call the word "the" the definite article

What do we call the words "a" and "an"?

We call the words "a" and "an" the indefinite articles

What's the difference between "a" and "an"?

The difference ... we use "a" ... consonant sound, whereas we use "an" ... vowel sound

Give me some examples, please.

a book, a university, an apple, an hour etc.

Use of the indefinite articles: "a" and "an"

countable   uncountable

The indefinite articles "a" and "an" mean the same as "one", and we use them with singular countable nouns. For example, we say "a chair", "an apple" etc. We do not use them with uncountable nouns like "bread", "water" etc.

When do we use the indefinite articles "a" and "an"?

We use the indefinite articles "a" and "an" with singular countable nouns

642 Give me some examples, please.

a table, an address etc.

Sometimes, we use the word "one" instead of the indefinite article, but only when we need to emphasize the number. For example, "I have two sisters but only <u>one</u> brother", or "There's just <u>one</u> problem with your idea of going to the cinema; we have no money". If we do not need to emphasize the number, we use the indefinite article. For example, "I went to a really good restaurant last night", or "He is an artist".

When do we use the word "one" instead of the indefinite article?

We use ... when we want to emphasize the number

Give me a sentence with the word "one", please.

I like one song on that CD but all the others are really boring

worm	silkworm	silk

What kind of worms are there?   There are earthworms, silkworms, woodworms etc.

What kind of things are often made of silk?   Ties, scarves etc. are often ...

limb

How many limbs do humans have?   Humans have four limbs

poison

If you discovered rats in your house, would you consider using poison to kill them?   Yes, if I ..., I'd consider ...
~ No, if I ..., I wouldn't consider ...

643 **cave**   **bat**

Would you be willing to spend a night alone in a cave full of bats?
Yes, I'd be ... ~ No, I wouldn't be ...

deserve

Do you think some people deserve more of the good things in life than others?   Yes, I think some people ...
~ No, I don't think some people ...

Why or why not?

Is there anything you think you deserve but have never received?
Yes, there is something I think I ...
~ No, there isn't anything I think I ...

What? Why?

fre<u>quent</u> (verb) **<u>fre</u>quent** (adjective) **<u>fre</u>quently** (adverb)

The word "fre<u>quent</u>" is a verb, whereas the word "<u>fre</u>quent" is an adjective.

What's the difference between the words "fre<u>quent</u>" and "<u>fre</u>quent"?

The difference ... is that ...

Do you frequent any clubs?

Yes, I frequent ...
~ No, I don't frequent ...

Do you pay frequent visits to your doctor?

Yes, I pay frequent ...
~ No, I don't pay frequent ...

How frequently do you visit your dentist?

I visit my
dentist about ...

644 **attract**   **attraction**   **attractive**

attention   **good-looking**

What's the best way to attract people's attention in the street?

The best way ... is to
shout loudly to them and wave

What are the main attractions of the place where you live?

The main attractions ...

Tell me the name of a famous person who you think is attractive even though they are not particularly beautiful or good-looking.

A famous person ... is ...

the rest

Do you think most people these days are too busy with their own lives to care about the rest of the people in the world?   Yes, I think most
people ... ~ No, I don't think most people ...

miserable

What kind of things make you feel miserable?

The kind
of things that ... are ...

Which do you think's the most miserable place on earth?

I think ...
is the most ...

Why?

645 What do we mean by "miserable weather"?   By "miserable weather"
we mean cold and rainy weather

emotion	**emotional**

Name some different emotions, please.

> Some different
> emotions are happiness,
> sadness, surprise, anger etc.

Do you ever get very emotional when you watch a sad film?

> Yes, I sometimes ... ~ No, I never ...

Idiom 19

look before you leap = think carefully before you make a big decision

e.g. You should always look before you leap when buying a house.

What does the idiom "look before you leap" mean?

> The idiom ...
> "think carefully ..."

Give me an example, please.

> Look before you leap;
> it will be too late after it's done

 Dictation 78

His member of parliament/ did everything in his power/ to save the man,/ but all to no purpose./ Smoking is not allowed in this building./ She tied her hair back/ so she could see better./ With the verb "to tell",/ we indicate the person/ that we are speaking to./ He told me/ everything that had happened/ during his holiday./ "To rock" can mean/ to move backwards and forwards.

 *Do Revision Exercise 52*

LESSON 119

"To be" + infinitive with "to"

firstly   secondly   head teacher   study

In formal English, there are two common uses of the structure "to be" + infinitive with "to".

Firstly, we use it in order to communicate an arrangement. For example, the sentence "The President is to meet the Queen" means that this meeting has been arranged. This structure is often used in newspapers (instead of the structure "going to").

Secondly, we can use this structure to communicate an obligation. For example, the sentence "You are to go to the head teacher's study at once" means you have to go to the head teacher's study at once. It is an obligation.

What are two common uses of the structure "to be" + infinitive with "to"?
Two common uses ... are to communicate an arrangement or an obligation

Give me some examples, please.
The two countries are to begin new discussions on trade. You are to wait until I get back.

What does this sentence mean: "The Prime Minister is to speak to the press at noon"?
That sentence means that there is an arrangement for the Prime Minister to speak to the press at noon

And what does this sentence mean: "The nurse said I was to wait for the doctor to come"?
That sentence means that the nurse told me that I had to wait for the doctor to come

647 **vote**

How old must you be before you can vote in elections in this country?

You must be ... before you can ...

nurse	**nursery**

What am I doing?

You're nursing your elbow

Have you ever had to nurse a sick person?

Yes, I've had to ...
~ No, I've never had to ...

What's a nursery, or nursery school?

A nursery, or
nursery school, is a place for very small
children to play while their parents go to work

unemployment

What is unemployment?

Unemployment is when
there's not enough work for everyone

What happens to the unemployed in your country?

The unemployed
in my country ...

take off   **land**   **seat belt**

What do passengers have to do when a plane takes off and lands?

Passengers have to put on their
seat belts when a plane takes off and lands

648 **practice**   **theory**   **practical**

take into account

What's the opposite of "theory"?

The opposite ... "practice"

Is it always possible to put theory into practice?

No, it isn't ...

Why not?

Because what works in theory
might not work in practice, because of
something that has not been taken into account

What do we mean by a practical person?

By a practical
person we mean someone who is good
at doing things with their hands, or is good at
organizing their ideas and making things happen in real life

set up

If you decided to set up a business in the place where you lived, what kind of business would you choose?

If I decided to set up ..., the kind of business I'd choose would be ...

Why?

"Could" as the past of "can"

We use "could" as the past of "can" to speak about general abilities. For example, we say "I could swim when I was five years old" or "When he lived in London, he could practise his English every day". On the other hand, if we talk about a particular occasion when somebody managed to do something, we don't use "could"; we use "was able", "managed" or "succeeded" instead. For example, we say "John studied a lot, and was able to pass the exam" or "The child fell into the swimming pool but managed to get out safely".

649 When do we use "could" as the past of "can"?

We use "could" as the past of "can" to speak about general abilities

Give me an example, please.

My grandfather could run very fast when he was a young man

When don't we use "could" as the past of "can"?

We don't ... if we talk about a particular occasion when somebody managed to do something

What do we use instead?

We use "was able", "managed" or "succeeded" instead

Give me an example, please.

The woman gave the children some money, and so they were able to buy some sweets

When a sentence is negative, however, we can use either "couldn't" or "wasn't able". We can say, for example, "He looked for his keys for a long time but he couldn't find them".

What happens when a sentence is negative?

When a sentence is negative, we can use either "couldn't" or "wasn't able"

Give me an example, please.

The woman did not
give the children any money,
and so they could not buy any sweets

nature   human nature

Is it in your nature to worry about things too much?

Yes, it's in ...
~ No, it isn't in ...

Do you think human nature can be changed?

Yes, I think ...
~ No, I don't think ...

650 ## compete   competition

Do you think it's a good thing to make children compete against each
other at school?

Yes, I think it's ...
~ No, I don't think it's ...

Have you ever won a competition?

Yes, I've won ...
~ No, I've never won ...

energy   efficient

Are you full of energy at the moment?

Yes, I'm full of ...
~ No, I'm not full of ...

What do we mean if we say that a person or machine works efficiently?

If we say ..., we mean that the person or
machine works well, without wasting time or energy

Are the cars that people drive today more efficient than the cars of fifty
years ago?

Yes, the cars that ...

suit   suitable

What colour clothes do you think suit you best?

I think ...
clothes suit me best

Would it suit you if you were asked to come to school on a public holiday?

Yes, it'd suit me if ...
~ No, it wouldn't suit me if ...

Why or why not?

Where would you say was the most suitable place to go for a holiday if you wanted a complete rest?

I'd say ...
was the most suitable ...

651 | **effect** | **perfect** | **to go up to**

What are the effects of too little sleep (or overeating etc.)?

The effects of ... are ...

Do you think regular physical exercise can have any effect on how happy someone feels?

Yes, I think ... ~ No, I don't think ...

What effect do you suppose it'd have on a perfect stranger if you went up to him in the street and hit him with a rolled-up newspaper?

If I went up to ..., I suppose the effect
it would have on him would be one of surprise

Idiom 20

drop a line = write a short letter

e.g. Don't forget to drop us a line while you're away.

What does the idiom "drop a line" mean?

The idiom ...
"write a short letter"

Give me an example, please.

Why didn't you drop us a
line to tell us you were coming?

sunshine

 Dictation 79

I'd like to live on an island/ right in the middle/ of the Pacific Ocean,/ but I realize/ that such an idea is only a dream./ It'd be very unwise/ to tell him the whole story/ during the interview;/ he might get the wrong idea./ We'll drive down to the coast/ early in the morning,/ so that we can get there by noon/ and spend a longer time/ enjoying the sunshine on the beach.

LESSON 120

"Should" and "ought to" for the past and future

We express the idea of past time with the modals "should" and "ought to" by following them with the word "have" and a past participle. For example, we say "I should have told her, but I forgot" or "He ought to have gone to the doctor yesterday, but he didn't". Notice that, if we say someone "should have done" or "ought to have done" something, it means that they did not, in fact, do it. The sentence "You should have phoned me" means that you did not, in fact, phone me.

How do we express the idea of past time with the modals "should" and "ought to"?

We express ... by following them with the word "have" and a past participle

Give me an example, please.

They ought to have gone to the police after the accident, but they didn't

Is there anything you should have done yesterday but didn't do?

Yes, there's ... ~ No, there isn't ...

If so, what?

What do I mean if I say that I ought to have called my mother yesterday?

If you say that ..., it means that you did not, in fact, call her

To express a future idea with "should" or "ought to", we just use a word or phrase that expresses future time. For example, "I ought to go and see him tomorrow".

How do we express a future idea with "should" or "ought to"?

We express a future ... by using a word or phrase that expresses future time

653 Give me some examples, please.

She should do it as soon as possible. They ought to arrive next week.

Is there anything you know you should do tomorrow but perhaps won't do?

Yes, there's something ... ~ No, there isn't anything ...

If so, what?

polish

When your shoes are dirty, do you just clean them or do you polish them as well?

> When my shoes are dirty, I ...

ability

Do you have any special ability that most people don't have?

> Yes, I have a ... ~ No, I don't have any ...

expense

What's the biggest expense in your daily life?

> The biggest ... is ...

postpone

What does the verb "to postpone" mean?

> The verb ... to delay something until a better time

Why are football matches sometimes postponed?

> Football matches ... due to bad weather

stress   stressful

Do you think people suffer from stress more these days than they used to?

> Yes, I think ... ~ No, I don't think ...

Name some situations that people normally find stressful.

> Some situations that ... are arguments, examinations, job interviews etc.

afterwards

The word "afterwards" expresses the idea of "after that". For example, "Shall we have dinner now? Afterwards, we can watch a film on TV if you like".

What does the word "afterwards" express?　　　The word "afterwards"
expresses the idea of "after that"

Give me an example, please.　　　They got married,
but separated soon afterwards

first of all

When we're painting a room, what is it important to do first of all?
When we're ..., first of all it's important
to cover the furniture so that it doesn't get paint on it

attend　　　　　　　　shopkeeper

Until what age must a child attend school?　　　A child must
attend school until the age of ...

Why should shopkeepers always try to be polite when they attend to
customers?　　　Shopkeepers should ... because
they want the customers to come back again

655　Do you attend to everything the teacher says during the lesson?　　Yes, I
attend to ... ~ No, I don't attend to ...

move　　　　　　　　tear

What would you say was the most moving event you've ever seen?
I'd say the most ... was ...

What kind of things move people to tears?　　　The kind of things that ...
are music, sad films, weddings etc.

Making requests　　　　pass

There are many ways of requesting that somebody does something, but
one common way is to say "Can you ...?" or "Could you ...?" In a request,
"could" is more polite than "can", and so we often use "could" when we
are speaking to people we don't know very well. For example, we say
"Excuse me, could you tell me the way to the station, please?"

Tell me one common way of making a request, please.　　　One common
way ... is to say "Can you ...?" or "Could you ...?"

Which is more polite: "can" or "could"?　　　"Could" is
more polite than "can"

Give me an example, please.

> Could you possibly lend me
> your pen for a second, please?

Another common way of making a request is to say "Do you mind ...?" or "Would you mind ...?" For example, "Do you mind opening the window, please?" or "Would you mind moving your chair a little, please?" The difference is that "Would you mind ...?" is perhaps more polite. Notice that we put a gerund after the verb "mind" in this type of request.

656 Tell me another common way of making a request, please.

> Another common way ... is to say
> "Do you mind ...?" or "Would you mind ...?"

Would you say: "Do you mind ...?" or "Would you mind ...?" if you wanted to be especially polite?

> I would say
> "Would you mind ...?" if I ...

Give me an example, please.

> Would you mind
> passing me that book, please?

spoil – spoilt – spoilt   discipline

What'd you do if you wanted to spoil someone's pleasure in eating their lunch?

> If I wanted to ..., I'd talk
> about something unpleasant

Do spoilt children usually lack discipline?

> Yes, spoilt children ...

hunger   share

If you were dying of hunger, would you share your last piece of food with another dying person?

> Yes, if I were ...,
> I'd ... ~ No, if I were ..., I wouldn't ...

Why do brothers and sisters often share bedrooms when they're young?

> Brothers and sisters ...
> because there aren't enough bedrooms,
> they're afraid of sleeping on their own in the dark etc.

Have you got any shares in any companies?

> Yes, I've got some ...
> ~ No, I haven't got any ...

Idiom 21

I don't know if I'm coming or going = I am confused (usually because different things are happening at the same time)

e.g. I've got so many problems and so much work to do that I just don't know if I'm coming or going.

What does the idiom "I don't know if I'm coming or going" mean?

The idiom ... "I am confused"

Give me an example, please.

Don't ask her to help; she's so busy that she doesn't know if she's coming or going at the moment

 *Do Revision Exercise 53*

LESSON 121

658 <u>**"Need" as a modal verb**</u>

The verb "need" can sometimes be used as a modal verb in questions and negative sentences (but not normally in positive sentences). For example, instead of asking "Does she need to fill in a form?", we can ask "Need she fill in a form?", and instead of saying "You don't need to pay the bill yet", we can say "You needn't pay the bill yet".

Give me an example of need as a modal verb in a question.

Need he come to work next Saturday?

Give me an example of need as a modal verb in a negative sentence.

She needn't worry about the exam

Need you look at your book to answer this question?   No, I needn't look ...

Need he/she help you to answer this question?

No, he/she
needn't help me ...

When talking about the past, if somebody says that they needn't have done something, it means that they did it, but it was, in fact, not necessary. For example, if a person says "I needn't have studied so hard, because the exam was really easy", it means that they <u>did</u> study hard, but it wasn't necessary. However, if somebody says that they didn't need to do something, it simply means that the action was not necessary, but it is not clear whether they did it or not.

What does somebody mean if they say that they needn't have done something?

If somebody says that ...,
it means that they did it, but
it was, in fact, not necessary

659 Tell me something you did yesterday that you needn't have done.

I needn't have carried an umbrella yesterday

So why did you?

Because ...

association — automobile

What kind of associations are there?

> There are automobile associations, football associations etc.

Do you belong to any associations?

> Yes, I belong to ...
> ~ No, I don't belong to ...

If so, which?

disturb — concentrate

Does every little noise disturb you when you're reading?

> Yes, every little noise disturbs ...
> ~ No, not every little noise disturbs ...

Why or why not?

> Because I can't concentrate ...
> ~ Because I can concentrate in spite of the noise

courage — virtue

Do you think it takes a lot of courage to act on the stage?

> Yes, I think ... ~ No, I don't think ...

Why is courage considered by some people the greatest of all the virtues?

> Courage is considered ...
> because one needs it to be
> able to practise the other virtues

660 loyal — loyalty

What do we mean by being loyal to someone?

> By being loyal to someone, we mean that we are true and faithful to them and give them our support

What's the noun of the adjective "loyal"?

> The noun of the adjective "loyal" is "loyalty"

companion

Which animal is man's most loyal companion?

> The dog is ...

spirit	spiritual	evil

What's the right spirit to adopt when learning a language?

The right spirit ... is that it's better
to speak and make a mistake than not to
speak because of being afraid of making a mistake

Where does a Christian hope his spirit will go to after death?

A Christian ... to heaven after death

Do you believe in evil spirits?

Yes, I believe in ...
~ No, I don't believe in ...

**What kind of things put you in high spirits and what kind of things put
you in low spirits?**

The kind of things that put me in
high spirits are ..., and the kind ... are ...

Do you drink spirits?

Yes, I drink ... ~ No, I don't drink ...

Would you say you were a spiritual person?

Yes, I'd say ...
~ No, I wouldn't say ...

661   **flow**

Which river flows through London?

The River Thames flows ...

Does traffic flow smoothly during the rush hour?

No, traffic
doesn't ...

festival	feast

**A festival is a large public party, often to celebrate something. For example,
a music festival, summer festival etc. A feast is a special meal, usually to
celebrate something. For example, there is usually a feast at a wedding.**

What's a festival?

A festival is ...

Have you ever been to a big music festival?

Yes, I've ...
~ No, I've never ...

What's a feast?

A feast is ...

662 **The verb "dare" means "to be brave enough to do something". For example, "Nobody dared to argue with him". It is often used in the negative. For example, "They didn't dare to walk through the woods at night".**

Would you dare to swim in the sea in the middle of winter?
> Yes, I would dare to swim ...
> ~ No, I wouldn't dare to swim ...

The verb "dare", like the verb "need", can be used as both an ordinary verb and a modal verb. For example, instead of asking "Do you dare to try it?", we can ask "Dare you try it?", and instead of saying "She doesn't dare to tell her father what happened", we can say "She daren't tell her father what happened". As a modal verb, "dare" is generally only used in questions and negative sentences, not in positive sentences.

Can the verb "dare" be used as both an ordinary verb and a modal verb?
> Yes, the verb "dare" ...

What can we say instead of "He doesn't dare to argue with his boss"?
> Instead of saying "He doesn't dare to argue with his boss", we can say "He daren't argue with his boss"

If we dare somebody to do something, it means that we challenge them to do it, to see if they are brave enough. For example, "I dare you to climb that tree". Note that when the verb "dare" is used with this meaning, it cannot be used as a modal verb.

If I dared you to jump out of a first-floor window, would you do it?
> Yes, if you dared me to jump ..., I'd do it
> ~ No, if you dared me to jump ..., I wouldn't do it

bring up

Where were you brought up?   I was brought up in ...

Do you believe children were brought up to be more polite in the past?
> Yes, I believe ... ~ No, I don't believe ...

solve   **calculator**

Is it difficult for most people to solve mathematical problems without
using a calculator?   Yes, it's difficult ...

663   **fix**   **hammer**   **nail**   **fingernail**

What'd one need in order to fix two pieces of wood together?
                                                    One would need a
                                        hammer and some nails to fix ...

When you pay a visit to the doctor's or dentist's, do you generally have to
fix an appointment before going or can you just go whenever you like?
                                                    When I pay a ...,
                                              I generally have to fix ...

What'd you have to do in order to fix a picture up on that wall?
                                        In order to ..., I'd need to hammer a nail
                                        into the wall and hang the picture on the nail

What's this?   It's a fingernail

criticize

If you went to a dinner party at somebody's house and criticized their
cooking, would you expect to be invited back again?
                                              No, if I went ..., I wouldn't ...

Idiom 22

fall to pieces = lose control of yourself and your emotions after something bad
has happened

e.g. He fell to pieces when his girlfriend left him, and didn't go to work for a
     whole week.

What does the idiom "fall to pieces" mean?   The idiom ...
                                                    "lose control ..."

Give me an example, please.   She was so shaken by the
                                        news that she just fell to pieces and
                                        was totally unable to manage the situation

Sometimes a university student/ can take quite a long time/ to gain a degree./ She checked out of the hotel/ but left her luggage in the reception./ My mark in mathematics/ was six out of ten,/ which is not too bad/ considering I had not studied too hard./ Some companies have very good trademarks,/ whilst others have trademarks/ that never really catch the eye./ On what basis/ could such an unwise decision/ have been made?

LESSON 122

665 **yard   courtyard   enclose   space**

Apart from being a measure of distance, the word "yard" can mean an open space outside a building, enclosed by walls, but with no roof. It is generally used for a special purpose. For example, a farmyard, a schoolyard, a railway yard, a backyard of a house etc.

Apart from being a measure of distance, what can the word "yard" mean?

> Apart from ..., the word "yard" can mean an open space outside a building, enclosed by walls, but with no roof

Give me some examples, please.

> Farmyard, schoolyard, railway yard ...

What is a "backyard"?

> A "backyard" is an enclosed space behind a house

A courtyard, on the other hand, is a large space, often enclosed by buildings, and is usually found in colleges, castles or very large houses.

What's a courtyard?

> A courtyard is ... and is usually found in colleges, castles or very large houses

amuse   comic   pass (the time)

cards   waiting room   amusement

What do people do when they are amused by a comic story?

> When people are amused by ... they laugh or smile

666 **The expression "to amuse yourself" means to pass the time, especially when you have nothing else to do. For example, "While we were waiting for the train, we amused ourselves by playing cards".**

What does the expression "to amuse yourself" mean?

> The expression "to amuse yourself" means ...

Give me an example, please.

While I was waiting to see the doctor, I amused myself by studying the other people in the waiting room, trying to see what they might be thinking from the expression on their faces

What kind of amusements are there in your home town?

In my home town, there are amusements such as cinemas, theatres etc.

hobby   photography

What's a hobby?

A hobby is a regular activity that people do in their free time for their own amusement rather than for making money

Can photography be an expensive hobby?   Yes, photography can ...

order

Why do some people arrange their CDs or books in alphabetical order on the shelf?   Some people ...
so that they are easy to find

pack   packed   suitcase   shorts   T-shirt

Name some things that people always pack in their suitcase when they go on holiday to a hot country.   Some things that ...
are shorts, T-shirts, sunglasses etc.

667 Do you like watching a film in a packed cinema?   Yes, I like ...
~ No, I don't like ...

thorn   rose

Name me a flower that's protected by thorns.   The rose is
a flower that's ...

afford

What do we mean when we say we can't afford to do something?

When we say we ... we mean we haven't got enough time or money to do it

Can most people afford to eat in restaurants every day?   No, most
people can't ...

If you were offered five free hours of English lessons a day, could you afford the time to take them?

Yes, if I were …, I could afford …

~ No, if I were …, I couldn't afford …

agreement

Do countries always respect the agreements they make with other countries?

No, countries don't always …

basket   trolley

When you do the shopping, do you normally use a basket or a trolley?

When I do …, I normally …

nut

Are nuts good for the health?

Yes, nuts are …

668 ## regarding

Where could I find information regarding concerts and other events in this area?

You could … by looking in local newspapers, visiting websites etc.

material   duvet   cotton   leather

What kind of material are duvet covers generally made of?

Duvet covers … cotton

Why is leather a good material for making bags from?

Leather is … because it's soft but also very strong

convenience   convenient   inconvenience

inconvenient   dining room

Why is it a great convenience to have a kitchen near to a dining room?

It's a great … because there's less distance to carry the food

Is it important to you to have every modern convenience in your home?

Yes, it's important … ~ No, it isn't important …

Would it be convenient for you to come to school at 4 a.m.?

No, it wouldn't be convenient
for ...; it'd be inconvenient

sensitive   offend   criticism   thermometer

The two basic meanings of the word "sensitive" are "able to notice small changes" and "easily hurt or offended".

669 **A sensitive thermometer can measure very small changes in temperature. A sensitive person can be either a kind person who is good at noticing changes in how other people are feeling, or a person who is easily hurt or offended by criticism. If you have sensitive teeth, your teeth can hurt when you have very hot or very cold drinks.**

What are the two basic meanings of the word "sensitive"?

The two ... are "able to notice
small changes" or "easily hurt or offended"

What do we mean by a sensitive thermometer?

By a ..., we
mean a thermometer that can
measure very small changes in temperature

Are your eyes sensitive to bright light?

Yes, my eyes are ...
~ No, my eyes aren't ...

Is it important for teachers to be sensitive to their pupils' feelings?

Yes, it's important for ...

What do we mean if we say that somebody is very sensitive to criticism?

If we say ..., we mean that
they are easily hurt or offended by criticism

sensible   reasonable

When we are thinking about a person's behaviour, the opposite of the word "stupid" is "sensible". A sensible person behaves in a practical and reasonable manner. For example, it is sensible to look both ways before crossing a road, whereas it is stupid to cross a road without looking both ways. It is sensible to save money for the future rather than spend all your money immediately.

When we're speaking about a person's behaviour, what's the opposite of the word "stupid"?

When we're speaking ..., the opposite of the word "stupid" is "sensible"

Are you sensible with money?

Yes, I'm sensible ...
~ No, I'm not sensible ...

670 Is it sensible to run across the road without looking?

No, it isn't sensible to ...

Why not?

Because we could be hit by a car

shopping centre

Is there a big shopping centre in this town?

Yes, there's a ...
~ No, there isn't a ...

balance   add up

What am I doing?

You're balancing your pen on your finger

If you add up figures in an accounts book and find they don't balance, what must you do?

If you add up ..., you must add them up again

If we had £100 between us, and I took £75 and gave the balance to you, how much would you get?

If we had ..., I'd get £25

bind – bound – bound

Basically, the verb "to bind" means "to tie". For example, to bind a wound, to bind a book, to bind with a promise.

What is, basically, the meaning of the verb "to bind"?

Basically, the meaning ... is "to tie"

What are the three forms of "bind"?

The three forms of "bind" are "bind, bound, bound"

Idiom 23

hit the nail right on the head = say something that identifies a problem or situation exactly, or say something that is exactly right

e.g. He hit the nail right on the head when he pointed out that the problem had been caused by the managers, not the workers.

What does the idiom "hit the nail right on the head" mean?

The idiom ... "say something ..."

Give me an example, please.

He hit the nail right on the head, and then we could see the problem perfectly

 *Dictation 81*

When we are given the bill/ in a restaurant,/ the service charge is often included,/ but it depends on the individual restaurant./ He always takes/ two toothbrushes with him/ when he goes on a long journey,/ as he is afraid he might lose one./ Some people shouted "Congratulations!"/ and then everybody raised a glass/ and said "Cheers!"/ There's one thing I hate/ and that is people interfering/ with my plans for the weekend.

 *Do Revision Exercise 54*

LESSON 123

Use of the indefinite articles: "a" and "an" (continued)

The indefinite article "a" (or "an") is used when we use a noun for the first time. If we then refer to the same thing or person again, we normally use the definite article "the". For example, "Yesterday, I received <u>a</u> letter and <u>an</u> email. I haven't read <u>the</u> letter yet, but I have read <u>the</u> email".

When we use a noun for the first time in a conversation, do we use the article "a" or "the"?

> When we use ..., we use the article "a"

Give me an example, please.

> Hi Jessica. I've just bought a new computer, and a printer too!

If we then refer to the same thing or person again, do we normally use "a" or "the"?

> If we then refer ..., we normally use "the"

Give me an example, please.

> Hi Jessica. I've just bought a new computer, and a printer too! The computer is really good but I 'm not sure about the printer; it was very cheap.

We sometimes use the definite article "the" when we use a noun for the first time, but only when the speaker and the listener both know who or what is being talked about. For example, "Ah, Doctor Jones. Good morning. <u>The</u> woman who phoned yesterday has arrived for her appointment." Here, it is clear which woman we are talking about – the woman who phoned yesterday.

In which situation do we use the definite article "the" when we use a noun for the first time?

> We use the definite article "the" ... only when the speaker and the listener both know who or what is being talked about

Give me an example, please.

> The book which is on the table is yours

673 **Another use of the indefinite article "a" is when we talk about people's jobs. For example, we say "She wants to become <u>a</u> doctor", or "He works as <u>a</u> waiter".**

Do we use the indefinite article when we talk about people's jobs?

Yes, we use ...

Would you like to be a teacher?

Yes, I'd like ...
~ No, I wouldn't like ...

Do you know anyone who works as a waiter?

Yes, I know someone ...
~ No, I don't know anyone ...

note   **note down**   **take notes**   **notebook**

banknote   **key**   **keyboard**

Do you note down all the new English words you hear?

Yes, I note down ... ~ No, I don't note down ...

Do you take notes in a notebook during the lesson?

No, I don't take ...

Why not?

Because if I did, I couldn't give my full attention to what was being said

Do you note anything different about this room from last lesson?

Yes, I note something ...
~ No, I don't note anything ...

What colour are the banknotes of your country?

The banknotes of my country are ...

Can women normally sing higher notes than men can?

Yes, women can ...

Does each key on a piano keyboard play a different note?

Yes, each key ...

674 What's the difference between a note and a letter?

The difference ... is that a note is normally shorter than a letter and less formal

armour

Why did soldiers wear armour in the old days?

Soldiers wore ... to protect themselves in battle

spread

How can we prevent a fire from spreading?

We can prevent ... by making everything around it wet

all over

Do you think people are basically the same all over the world?

> Yes, I think people ... ~ No, I don't think people ...

fascinated

Have you ever visited a particular part of the world simply because you were fascinated by the local culture?

> Yes, I've ... ~ No, I've never ...

scene   murderer   evidence

Why do you think murderers sometimes return to the scene of their crime?

> I think murderers ... because they think
> that they may have left some evidence there

675 Can a court find someone guilty of a crime if there is no evidence?

> No, a court can't ...

i.e. = id est = that is

The letters "i.e." are the abbreviation of "id est", which is Latin for "that is". We use this abbreviation mainly in writing.

What are the letters "i.e." the abbreviation of?

> The letters "i.e."
> are the abbreviation of "id est" ... "that is"

When do we use this abbreviation?

> We use this
> abbreviation mainly in writing

Be used to something   Get used to something

at first   accustomed

Instead of saying "I played football regularly at school", we can use the auxiliary "used to" and say "I used to play football at school". This sentence expresses a habit or repeated action in the past.

However, we have another, completely different, "used to" in English. In the sentence "I am used to hot weather", the word "used" is an adjective, followed by the preposition "to". If we say that we are "used to" something, it means that it is not strange or uncomfortable for us

anymore because we have experience of it. If a person from a cold country goes to live in a hot country, at first they feel uncomfortable; they "are not used to" the weather. Then, they slowly become accustomed to the weather, or "get used to" the weather. Finally, one day they say "I am used to hot weather" because now they are comfortable with it.

What does it mean if we say that we are used to something?

> If we say that ..., it means that it is not strange or uncomfortable for us anymore because we have experience of it

676 Give me an example, please.

> He's lived on that busy street for many years, so he is used to the traffic noise

Is an African person used to hot weather?

> Yes, an African person is used to hot weather

Why?

> Because it is hot in Africa, and if someone is born and brought up there, hot weather is normal for them

When a family moves to a new town, do you think it's easier for the children to get used to everything than it is for the parents?

> Yes, when a family moves ..., I think ...
> ~ No, when a family moves ..., I don't think ...

Notice that, because the word "to" is a preposition, we put the gerund ("-ing" form) after the expression "to be used to", not the infinitive. For example, we say "I am getting used to waking up early".

Why do we put the gerund after the expression "to be used to"?

> We put ... because the word "to" is a preposition

Give me an example, please.

> At first it was difficult, but now I'm used to getting up early

Are you used to studying with the Callan Method?

> Yes, I'm used to studying ... ~ No, I'm not used to studying ...

Do you think you could ever get used to living in a country where your language wasn't spoken?

> Yes, I think I could ...
> ~ No, I don't think I could ever ...

Idiom 24

pull yourself together = gain control of yourself and your emotions after a difficult experience

e.g. He fell to pieces when his girlfriend left him, and it took him a few weeks to pull himself together again.

677 **What does the idiom "pull yourself together" mean?**

The idiom ...
"gain control of ..."

Give me an example, please.

Stop crying and pull yourself together!

Dictation 82

I should really do the work now;/ otherwise, I'll have twice as much/ to do later on./ I've seen that film/ on several occasions,/ but never on the big screen./ Whatever else happens during the day,/ I always keep to a set time/ for getting up,/ eating and going to bed,/ and so I always feel healthy./ In a civilized society,/ people show respect to others./ It is said/ that one should always practise/ what one preaches.

LESSON 124

678 **benefit**   **sake**   **give up**

What are the benefits of regular physical exercise?   The benefits ...
                                        are good health, more energy etc.

When arguing with someone, do you ever suddenly agree with them just
for the sake of peace and quiet?   Yes, when arguing ...,
                                        I sometimes suddenly ...
                                 ~ No, when arguing ..., I never suddenly ...

Do you think it's important for parents who smoke to try to give up
smoking for the sake of their children?   Yes, I think
                                        it's ... ~ No, I don't think it's ...

mixed up

If two people have very similar names, do you sometimes get them mixed
up?   Yes, if two people ..., I sometimes ...
                                 ~ No, if two people ..., I never ...

Which word am I spelling all mixed up? c–i–r–h–a   You're spelling
                                        the word "chair" all mixed up

humour

Do you think a sense of humour is one of the most important parts of a
person's character?   Yes, I think ... ~ No, I don't think ...

679 **dress**

Do people wear formal dress when they go to a wedding?   Yes, people
                                 wear formal dress when they go to a wedding

master   masterpiece

When discussing painting, who do we mean by the Old Masters?
                     When discussing painting, by the Old Masters
                 we mean painters such as Rembrandt, Michelangelo etc.

Can you name me one of Shakespeare's masterpieces?

> Yes, I can name you one of Shakespeare's
> masterpieces – Hamlet (Macbeth, Othello, King Lear etc.)

How long do you think it would take you to master another foreign language (or the game of golf)?

> I think it'd take
> me about … to master …

"So" – and its many uses

so	**so that**	**so as to**	**and so on**

so many	**so far**	**so far as I know**

There are many expressions in English that contain the word "so". Here are some examples:

1) "They were very cheap, (and) <u>so</u> I bought two of them".
   Here, the word "so" means "therefore" or "consequently".

2) "You should read it again, <u>so that</u> you can remember it well".
   Here, the expression "so that" means "in order that".

3) "Come early, <u>so as to</u> get a good seat".
   Here, the expression "so as to" means "in order to".

680 4) "Everybody was at the party – Sam, Louise, Richard <u>and so on</u>".
   Here, the expression "and so on" means "etc".

Now, I will say a sentence and I want you to make a similar sentence with the word "so":

I had no money for the bus and consequently I had to walk home.

> I had … bus, so I had to …

I'll show you where the key is kept in order that you don't have to ask me next time.

> I'll show … kept so that you don't …

We wore very light clothes in order not to suffer from the heat.

> We wore … clothes so as not to suffer …

I went to the supermarket and bought some milk, cheese, bread etc.

> I went … cheese, bread and so on

Here are some more uses of "so":

5) "I never realized there were <u>so many</u> people living in that house".
Here, the expression "so many" means "such a large number of".
(For uncountable nouns, we use "so much", meaning "such a large quantity of".)

6) "I have not made any mistakes <u>so far</u>".
Here, the expression "so far" means "till now".

7) "<u>So far as I know</u>, they left yesterday".
Here, the expression "so far as I know" means "as regards my knowledge of the situation".

Now, as before, I will say a sentence and I want you to make a similar sentence with the word "so":

I never knew he had such a large quantity of money.
I never ... had so much money

681 I haven't had an accident in my car till now.
I haven't ... car so far

As regards my knowledge of the situation, the problem has been solved.
So far as I know, the problem ...

praise

Is it important for teachers to praise children when they do things well?
Yes, it's important for ...

What's the danger of giving children too much praise?
The danger ... is that they might think they are better than they really are and start to become careless in their work

loan

Is it easy to get a loan from a bank?
Yes, it's easy to ...
~ No, it isn't easy to ...

furthermore   moreover

The words "furthermore" and "moreover" mean "also", and are often used at the beginning of the sentence in formal English. For example, "The goods arrived two weeks late. Furthermore, they were damaged".

The word "moreover" often communicates that the information in the second sentence is more important than the information in the first. For example, "My boss praised me for my work yesterday. Moreover, he said he was going to pay me more money".

682 Give me an example of the word "furthermore", please.
                           Alison speaks French perfectly. Furthermore, she can communicate quite well in German.

Give me an example of the word "moreover", please.
                           The company make good products. Moreover, their prices are low.

toe

How many toes do you have?
                           I have ten toes

personally

Do you know any famous people personally?
                           Yes, I know …
                           ~ No, I don't know …

Do sensitive people sometimes take criticism too personally?
                           Yes, sensitive people …

conscious   unconscious   self-conscious

patient   injection   gathering

When a person is in danger, do you think it's better for them to be conscious of the danger or not?
                         When a person …, I think it's better …

Why?

What do they give a hospital patient to make them unconscious before an operation?
                         They usually … a special kind of gas or an injection to make …

683 On what occasions do people often feel self-conscious?

People often feel self-conscious on occasions such as formal gatherings, or when they're with people they don't know

split	axe	equally

What do we use to split wood?

We use an axe to split wood

If your favourite trousers split, would you repair them or throw them away?

If my ..., I'd ...

When you eat in a restaurant with a group of friends, do you think the bill should be split equally among everyone or do you think each person should pay for what they personally ordered?

When I eat in ..., I think ...

Idiom 25

kill two birds with one stone = do two things at the same time and, therefore, save time and energy

e.g. When we go to the station to buy the tickets, let's ask about the train times for our next trip. By doing that, we can kill two birds with one stone.

What does the idiom "kill two birds with one stone" mean?

The idiom ... "do two things ..."

Give me an example, please.

If I can find the book I need for school at the library when I go there to return your books, I'll be killing two birds with one stone

 *Do Revision Exercise 55*

LESSON 125

684 **Uses of the definite article: "the"**

| Alps | Andes | Himalayas | Netherlands |

The most important use of the definite article "the" is when we are referring to something specific that is known to both the speaker and the listener. This is similar to the way that we use the words "this", "that", "these" or "those". For example, "The teacher we had last week has left", or "John's got a new house; the garden's lovely", or "The sun rose early today".

What is the most important use of the definite article "the"?

> The most important ... is when
> we are referring to something specific
> that is known to both the speaker and the listener

Give me some examples, please.

> The DVDs I bought yesterday are great.
> Could you close the window, please?
> The sky's grey today.

There are three other special uses of the definite article "the" that we should remember:

1) **We can sometimes use the word "the" to speak about things in general, but only when we are speaking about <u>types</u> of animals or <u>types</u> of things. For example, instead of saying "Tigers are dangerous animals", we can say "The tiger is a dangerous animal". This doesn't refer to one specific tiger, but to tigers in general. Instead of saying "Computers are very useful things", we can say "The computer is a very useful thing". This means computers in general.**

How can we sometimes use the word "the" to speak about things in general?

> We can sometimes use the word
> "the" to speak about things in general when
> we are speaking about <u>types</u> of animals or <u>types</u> of things

685 Which is the heaviest land animal on earth?

> The elephant is ...

When was the mobile phone invented?

> The mobile phone
> was invented in 1973

2) We sometimes put the definite article "the" in front of a name, but only when it is the name of a river, sea, ocean or mountain chain. For example "the Thames", "the Mediterranean", "the Atlantic", "the Alps" etc. We do not use "the" with the names of people and places. For example, we say "Queen Elizabeth lives in London".

When do we put the definite article "the" in front of a name?

> We put the definite article "the"
> in front of a name when it is the name
> of a river, sea, ocean or mountain chain

Give me some examples of mountain chains.

> Some examples ...
> are the Andes, the Himalayas, the Alps etc.

Which is the longest river in the world?

> The Nile is ...

3) Finally, we occasionally put the word "the" in front of the name of a country, but only if the name is plural in form. For example, "the Netherlands", "the United States of America" etc. With country names that are singular in form, we do not use "the". For example, we say "France" (not "the France").

When do we put the word "the" in front of the name of a country?

> We put the word "the" in front of the
> name of a country only if the name is plural in form

Name some countries that are plural in form, please.

> The Netherlands,
> the United States of America etc.

present /ˈprezənt/	**present** /prɪˈzent/
(noun + adjective)	(verb)

Do you think that the present state of the world is better than a hundred years ago?

> Yes, I think ... ~ No, I don't think ...

686 Why or why not?

Were all the pupils present for the last lesson?

> Yes, all the pupils ...
> ~ No, not all the pupils ...

When a person retires from work after many years of employment in the same company, are they usually presented with a gift?   Yes,
                                                                          when a person ...

In job interviews, are people sometimes judged more by the way they present themselves than by their abilities and experience?   Yes, in
                                                                 job interviews, people are ...

Do you enjoy choosing presents to give to other people or do you find it stressful?   I enjoy choosing ... ~ I find choosing ...

swear – swore – sworn

The verb "to swear" means to say bad words. People often swear when they hurt themselves or when they're very angry.

What does the verb "to swear" mean?   The verb "to swear" ...

What are the three forms of "swear"?   The three forms of
                                                       "swear" are "swear, swore, sworn"

When do people swear?   People swear when ...

Are there some people who have never sworn in their lives?   Yes,
                                                                       there are ...

687 **lazy**   **idle**

The word "lazy" means "not willing to work". For example, "My brother is so lazy; he does nothing all day!" The word "idle" usually means the same as "lazy", but only when we are describing people. For example, "Don't be so idle. Go and find a job!"

Who's the laziest person you know?   The laziest ...

Does hot weather make you feel lazy?   Yes, hot weather makes ...
                                                    ~ No, hot weather doesn't make ...

When we're describing people, what's another word for "lazy"?
                                                  When we're ..., another word ... "idle"

When we are describing things, the word "idle" means "not doing anything". For example, "The ship remained idle in the port for two years". We can sometimes use "idle" with this meaning for people but it is not very common. For example, "I hate to be idle at work; I always like to be doing something useful".

When we're describing things, what does the word "idle" mean?

> When we're ..., the word ... "not doing anything"

If you parked a car outside your house and left it idle for a few months, would it get very dirty?

> Yes, if I parked a car ..., it'd get ...

What do I mean if I say "The workers were idle because the machines had broken down"?

> If you say ..., you mean they were not doing anything because ...

play   scene

When was the last time you went to see a play at the theatre?

> The last time I ... was ...

688 Why do we always remember certain scenes in a film better than we remember others?

> We always remember ... because they are very emotional or full of action

verse   chorus

Are Shakespeare's plays written mainly in verse?

> Yes, Shakespeare's plays are written mainly in verse

What do we call a part of a song that is repeated more than once: a verse or a chorus?

> We call ... a chorus

pray   prayer

How do people pray, and what do they usually say in their prayers?

> People often pray with their eyes closed, and they usually ask for something in their prayers

combine

Tell me the name of a job that you think combines work and pleasure.

> The name of ...

Idiom 26

go in one ear and out the other = be heard but then immediately forgotten

e.g. There's no use telling him anything; it just goes in one ear and out the other.

What does the idiom "go in one ear and out the other" mean?

The idiom ... "be heard ..."

689 **Give me an example, please.**

I've told my son a hundred times
not to go out without his coat on,
but it goes in one ear and out the other

heads   **tails**

 Dictation 83

One side of a coin/ we call "heads",/ and the other side/ we call "tails"./ Totally by accident,/ he knocked the glass/ containing the liquid/ off the table/ onto the floor./ His lips rarely part/ to show his teeth,/ even when he smiles broadly./ The poor bird could hardly fly,/ as one of its wings/ was badly damaged./ Before the battle began,/ it was expected that many of the sailors/ would fail to do their duty,/ and that, consequently,/ the battle would be lost.

LESSON 126

690 **extend**   **as far as**

How far does the road outside this window extend?   The road outside
this window extends as far as ...

Extend your arms towards the ceiling, please.

What are you doing?   I'm extending my ... .

Future time clauses

As we know, we cannot use future verb forms in time clauses; we use
present verb forms instead. We cannot say "When I will eat dinner, I will
watch TV". We must say either

"When I <u>eat</u> dinner, I will watch TV"

or

"When I <u>have eaten</u> dinner, I will watch TV".

If I use the present simple and say "When I <u>eat</u> dinner, I will watch TV", it
is possible that the two actions will happen at the same time or one after
the other. On the other hand, if I use the present perfect and say "When I
<u>have eaten</u> dinner, I will watch TV", I am emphasizing that I will first eat
dinner and then, after that, I will watch TV.

691 Tell me the difference between these two sentences:

"When she <u>writes</u> the letter, she will drink a coffee"
and

"When she <u>has written</u> the letter, she will drink a coffee".

The difference between these two sentences is that "When she
<u>writes</u> the letter, she will drink a coffee" means that it is possible that
the two actions will happen at the same time or one after the other,
whereas "When she <u>has written</u> the letter, she will drink a coffee"
means that she will write first and then, after that, drink

trust

Is there anyone you can think of who you could trust with your life?

Yes, there's someone ...
~ No, there isn't anyone ...

Do you think it's a good idea for parents to put money in a trust for their children so that the children can only use it when they reach a certain age?

Yes, I think it's ... ~ No, I don't think it's ...

dependent   independent

When you were a young child, were you completely dependent on your parents for everything?

Yes, when I was ...

When did the United States of America become independent from Britain?

The United States ...
on the 4th of July, 1776

692 punctual

Why is it important to be punctual when you have an appointment with your doctor or dentist?

It's important ...
because they might not be
able to see you if you arrive late

row   oar

In the old days before steam, ships were made to move either by rowing with oars, or by using a sail.

How were ships made to move in the old days before steam?

In the old days before steam, ships were ...

wish

We use the verb "wish" to communicate the idea that we would like things to be different from the way they in fact are now, or were in the past. For example, "I wish I were a millionaire".

What does the verb "wish" communicate? The verb "wish" communicates the idea that we would like things to be different from the way they in fact are now, or were in the past

We must remember that the tense of any verb that follows "wish" is one step back into the past from the time that we are referring to. So, instead of the present simple tense we use the past simple tense; for example, "Maria wishes she <u>spoke</u> perfect English" (she doesn't speak perfect English). Instead of the past simple tense we use the past perfect tense; for example, "Daniel wishes he <u>had gone</u> to the party last night" (he didn't go to the party). Instead of the present continuous tense we use the past continuous tense; for example, "I wish <u>it wasn't</u> raining" (it is raining).

693 What must we remember about the tense of any verb that follows "wish"? We must remember that the tense of any verb that follows "wish" is one step back into the past from the time that we are referring to

Give me an example, please. I wish I could fly

Do you have a million pounds? No, I don't have ...

Do you wish you had a million pounds? Yes, I wish I had ...
~ No, I don't wish I had ...

Are you relaxing on a beach at the moment? No, I'm not relaxing ...

Do you wish you were relaxing on a beach at the moment?
Yes, I wish I was relaxing ...
~ No, I don't wish I was relaxing ...

Did you meet a famous film star yesterday? No, I didn't meet ...

Do you wish you had met a famous film star yesterday? Yes, I wish I had met ... ~ No, I don't wish I had met ...

ideal	theoretical	actual	actually

Are you the kind of person who enjoys talking about the ideal, theoretical state of things, or do you consider such things a waste of time and prefer to talk about the actual state of things? I'm the kind of person who ...

694 Give me a sentence with the word "actually" in it.

He always used to say he was a good football player but, actually, he wasn't very good

check   change

If you gave a shopkeeper £10 for something that cost £5 and he gave you only £4 change, what would you do?

If I gave ..., I'd ...

When you pay for something in a shop, do you always check to see that they have given you the right change?

Yes, when I pay ...,
I always ... ~ No, when I pay ..., I don't always ...

Why or why not?

log   fireplace

Which would you prefer to sit in front of on a cold winter's day: a real log fire burning in the fireplace, or a modern gas fire?

On a cold ...,
I'd prefer to ...

common sense

What is common sense?

Common sense is practical good sense which is not gained from any special studies

Which is more important in everyday life: intelligence or common sense?

Common sense is more important ...

Why?

695 **tool**

Which tool would you need if you wanted to hit a nail into a piece of wood?

I'd need a hammer if I ...

bean

Are beans good for the health?

Yes, beans are ...

What do we mean when we say that someone's full of beans?

When we say ..., we mean
they're full of life and energy

Idiom 27

cut corners = do something quickly and not as well as you could

e.g. The new road is not very smooth because the workmen obviously cut
corners to get it finished quickly.

What does the idiom "cut corners" mean?

The idiom ...
"do something quickly ..."

Give me an example, please.

There wasn't enough
money to complete the job
properly, so we had to cut corners

 *Do Revision Exercise 56*

Grammar Questions

The following grammar questions are to be asked and revised in exactly the same way as any other questions in the Method. They act as a complete and rapid revision of all the grammar in Stages 7 and 8.

Stage 7

1) When the past tense of a regular verb ends in "ded" or "ted", how do we pronounce the final sound? Give me some examples.

> When the past tense of a regular verb ends in "ded" or "ted", we pronounce the final sound "id" /ɪd/. For example, "included", "lasted" etc.

2) When the past tense of a regular verb does not end in "ded" or "ted", how do we pronounce the final sound? Give me some examples.

> When the past tense of a regular verb does not end in "ded" or "ted", we pronounce the final sound "t" /t/ or "d" /d/. For example, "crossed", "seemed" etc.

3) What's the difference between "a few" and "few"?

> The difference between "a few" and "few" is that "a few" simply means "not many", whereas "few" often expresses the idea of "not enough" or "fewer than expected".

4) What's the difference between "a little" and "little"?

> The difference between "a little" and "little" is that "a little" simply means "not much", whereas "little" often expresses the idea of "not enough" or "less than expected".

5) When do we use the words "used to", and what does it mean? Give me an example.

> We use the words "used to", for a habit or repeated action in the past, especially when the action is now finished. For example, "I used to go to the cinema a lot when I was a child".

6) What's the difference between "we're going to go to the theatre" and "we're going to the theatre"?

> The difference between "We're going to go to the theatre" and "We're going to the theatre" is that "We're going to go to the theatre" communicates that it is our intention to go, whereas "We're going to the theatre" communicates that the visit has already been arranged; we already have the tickets, for example.

7) **How do we make the question form in English? Give me an example.**

We make the question form in English by putting the subject after the first auxiliary verb. For example, the statement "She has been eating" becomes "Has she been eating?"

8) **For the present simple and the past simple, which auxiliary verb do we use in the question form? Give me an example.**

For the present simple and the past simple, we use the auxiliary verb "do" in the question form. For example, "Do you want some tea?"

9) **What's a clause? Give me an example.**

A clause is any group of words with a subject and a main verb. For example, "The door opened".

10) **What's a conjunction? Give me some examples.**

A conjunction is a word that joins clauses together to make long sentences. For example, "and", "because", "but", "so" and "if".

11) **Give me an example of a sentence that contains two clauses joined together by a conjunction.**

For example, "I love chocolate because it tastes so good".

12) **What's the difference between a main clause and a dependent clause?**

The difference between a main clause and a dependent clause is that a main clause contains the main message of the sentence whereas a dependent clause contains other information.

13) **Which is the main clause in this sentence? "If I don't sleep enough, I feel tired."**

"I feel tired" is the main clause in that sentence.

14) **And which is the dependent clause?**

"If I don't sleep enough" is the dependent clause.

15) **Which conjunctions cannot start a sentence?**

The conjunctions "and ", "or" and "but" cannot start a sentence.

16) **Give me an example of the construction "make + object + adjective".**

"Work makes us tired".

17) **Give me an example of the construction "keep + object + adjective".**

"Exercise keeps you healthy".

18) What is a relative clause? A relative clause is a clause that we use to describe a noun.

19) Where do we put a relative clause? We put a relative clause immediately after the noun it describes.

20) What's the difference between "who", "which" and "that"? The difference between "who", "which" and "that" is that we use "who" for people, "which" for things and animals, and "that" for people, things and animals.

21) Give me a sentence with a relative clause in it. "I know someone who lives in that street". "The film that I saw yesterday was great".

22) When do we put the words "so", "neither" or "nor" at the beginning of a sentence? We put the words "so", "neither" or "nor" at the beginning of a sentence when someone makes a statement and we want to reply that the same situation is true for us or somebody else.

23) How do we make this kind of short reply? Give me some examples. We make this kind of short reply by using the words "so", "neither", or "nor", and by putting the auxiliary verb before the subject. For example, "I can speak English" – "So can I". "I won't go there" – "Neither will I".

24) If there is no auxiliary verb, which verb do we use? Give me an example. If there is no auxiliary verb, we use "do" in the short reply. For example, "He lives in this building" – "So does my sister".

25) What is a phrase? Give me an example. A phrase is a collection of words that belong together in a sentence because, together, they form a particular part of the sentence. For example, "at high speed".

26) What do we mean by a preparatory "it"? Give me some examples. By a preparatory "it" we mean that we use the word "it" at the beginning of a sentence to prepare us for some information that comes later in the sentence. For example, "It is very difficult to understand what he says"; "Was it usual for him to come here every Sunday?"; "It isn't common to find that kind of bird in this part of the country".

27) Why do we use the words "so" and "not" when replying to something that someone has just said? We use the words "so" and "not" when replying to something that someone has just said to avoid repeating the whole sentence.

28) Give me some examples of this use of the word "so".

"Is that right what James said?" –
"I'm afraid so"; "I hope so"; "I suppose so"; "I think so".

29) Give me some examples of the use of the word "not".

"Is that right what James said?" –
"I'm afraid not"; "I hope not"; "I suppose not".

30) When do we use the word "so" at the beginning of a sentence? Give me an example.

We use the word "so" at the beginning of a sentence when we already know something that someone has just told us. For example, someone says to us "Mr Jones has gone to Australia" and, knowing this fact, we reply "So we've been told".

31) Why do we say "I ate eggs for breakfast today" and not "I have eaten eggs for breakfast today"?

We say "I ate eggs for breakfast today" because we are thinking about what happened at a specific past time – breakfast time. We are not thinking about now.

32) What are some common adverbs of frequency?

Some common adverbs of frequency are: "never", "rarely", "occasionally", "sometimes", "often", "usually" and "always".

33) Where do these adverbs normally go? Give me an example.

These adverbs normally go after the first auxiliary verb. For example, "I have never been to Australia" or "He will always love her".

34) If there is no auxiliary verb, where do these adverbs normally go? Give me an example.

If there is no auxiliary verb, these adverbs normally go directly before the verb. For example, "They rarely go to the theatre" or "Steve usually drinks beer".

35) If the verb is negative, where do these adverbs normally go? Give me an example.

If the verb is negative, these adverbs normally go after the word "not". For example, "He has not often spoken to us" or "I haven't always had long hair".

36) Where do adverbs such as "even" and "also" usually go? Give me some examples.   Adverbs such as "even" and "also" usually go in the same position as adverbs of frequency. For example, "I have also been reading that book" or "Sophie can speak several languages; she even speaks Chinese".

37) What do we do when we change a question from direct into indirect speech? Give me an example.   When we change a question from direct into indirect speech, we move the verb one step back into the past, we use "asked" instead of "said", and we do not use the question form or a question mark. For example, "I asked them what they wanted to drink".

38) If the question does not contain a question word, what do we use instead? Give me an example.   If the question does not contain a question word, we use the word "if" or "whether" instead. For example, "He asked her if (or whether) she spoke English".

39) What do we do when we change an imperative from direct into indirect speech? Give me an example.   When we change an imperative from direct into indirect speech, we use "told", "commanded" or "ordered", and we use the infinitive without "to" instead of the imperative. For example, "The king commanded him to leave".

40) With negative imperatives, what do we do? Give me an example.   With negative imperatives, we put "not" before the infinitive. For example, "His mum told him not to get home late".

41) What do we do when we change a request from direct into indirect speech? Give me an example.   When we change a request from direct into indirect speech, we use "asked", and we can use the same constructions that we use for indirect questions or imperatives. For example, "We asked them if they could show us the way" or "We asked them to show us the way".

42) Can we use future tenses in time clauses and conditional clauses?   No, we can't use future tenses in time clauses and conditional clauses.

43) What do we use instead? Give me some examples.

We use present tenses instead. For example, "She is going to buy a house in the countryside when she retires". "They will call me tomorrow if they have any problems".

44) What words can we use when we want to emphasize the person who does the action in a particular sentence?

When we want to emphasize the person who does the action in a particular sentence, we can use "myself", "yourself", "himself" etc.

45) What do we call these words?

We call these words emphasizing pronouns.

46) Give me three sentences containing emphasizing pronouns.

"I remember it very clearly, because I gave him the money myself". "People cannot usually repair laptops themselves; they have to take them to a computer repair centre". "She always drove the car herself".

47) What's the difference between these two sentences: "I did the translation myself" and "I did the translation by myself"?

The difference between these two sentences is that "I did the translation myself" emphasizes the fact that I did the translation and not someone else, whereas "I did the translation by myself" means that I did the translation alone, without any help.

48) What are the two types of relative clause?

The two types of relative clause are defining clauses and non-defining clauses.

49) What's the difference between defining clauses and non-defining clauses? Give me an example of each.

The difference between defining clauses and non-defining clauses is that defining clauses identify (or define) which person or thing we are talking about, whereas non-defining clauses do not identify a person or thing, but simply give us extra information about them. For example, "The milk that she bought this morning is in the fridge" and "My new glasses, which I bought yesterday, are really expensive".

50) How is a non-defining clause separated from the main part of the sentence?

A non-defining clause is separated from the main part of the sentence by commas.

51) When can we use the relative pronoun "that" instead of "who" or "which"? Give me an example. We can use the relative pronoun "that" instead of "who" or "which" in defining clauses; we cannot use "that" in non-defining clauses. For example, "The biscuits that I ate were very tasty".

Stage 8

52) When do we add the letters "es" to form the plural of a noun and the third person singular of a verb? Give me an example of each – both noun and verb. We add the letters "es" to form the plural of a noun and the third person singular of a verb when a word ends in one of the letters "o", "s", "x", "z", "ch" or "sh". For example, "One potato – two potatoes"; "I go – you go – he goes".

53) What happens when a noun or verb ends in a consonant plus "y"? Give me an example – both noun and verb. When a noun or verb ends in a consonant plus "y", the "y" is changed to "i" and then the letters "es" are added. For example, "one lady – two ladies"; "I cry – you cry – he cries".

54) How do we generally form the plural of a noun ending in "f" or "fe"? Give me an example We generally form the plural of a noun ending in "f" or "fe" by changing the "f" or "fe" to "ves". For example, "leaf – leaves".

55) What are three common exceptions to this rule? Three common exceptions to this rule are "chefs", "cliffs", and "roofs".

56) When do we use the present simple to speak about a future action? Give me an example. We use the present simple to speak about a future action when we are talking about timetables or schedules. For example, "My train leaves in fifteen minutes".

57) When do we use the relative pronoun "what"? Give me an example. We use the relative pronoun "what" when we don't mention the thing that the relative clause describes. For example, "She told the waiter what she wanted".

58) When do some people prefer to use the relative pronoun "whom" instead of "who"? Give me an example.

Some people prefer to use the relative pronoun "whom" instead of "who" with formal English, when the relative pronoun is not the subject of the verb that follows. For example, "The gentleman whom he informed was the manager".

59) When we have a preposition at the beginning of a relative clause, can we follow the preposition with the word "who"? Give me an example.

No, when we have a preposition at the beginning of a relative clause, we cannot follow the preposition with "who"; we must use "whom". For example, "We need to contact the customer from whom she took the payment".

60) When do we use the word "whose" at the beginning of a relative clause? Give me an example.

We use the word "whose" at the beginning of a relative clause instead of using a possessive adjective like "my", "your", "his" etc. For example, "The woman whose handbag was stolen is on her way to the police station".

61) What's the difference between a transitive verb and an intransitive verb?

The difference between a transitive verb and an intransitive verb is that a transitive verb has an object, whereas an intransitive verb does not have an object.

62) Give me some sentences containing transitive verbs.

The car hit the wall. The boy cut his thumb. They pushed the table. He opened the door.

63) Give me some sentences containing intransitive verbs.

The sun rises at 6 o'clock. He gets up very early in the morning. People walk very quickly in winter. The door opened.

64) Is the object of a transitive verb always stated? Give me an example.

No, the object of a transitive verb isn't always stated. For example, "He ate quickly".

65) Name some English nouns that are never used in the plural.

Some English nouns that are never used in the plural are "advice", "furniture", "information", "knowledge", "progress" and "news".

66) **How can we sometimes communicate a plural idea with nouns like this? Give me an example.** We can sometimes communicate a plural idea with nouns like this by using expressions such as "pieces of" or "items of". For example, "She gave him two pieces of valuable advice".

67) **How can we sometimes form a feminine noun from a masculine noun? Give me some examples.** We can sometimes form a feminine noun from a masculine noun by adding the letters "ess". For example, "actress", "hostess", "princess".

68) **What do we do with nouns when we use them in the general sense? Give me an example.** When we use nouns in the general sense, we put them in the plural and we do not put an article in front of them. For example, "People go to cinemas to watch films".

69) **What do we do if a noun doesn't have a plural form?** If a noun doesn't have a plural form, we simply use it on its own, also without an article. For example, "Paper comes from wood".

70) **What are the articles in English?** The articles in English are "the", "a" and "an".

71) **What do we call the word "the"?** We call the word "the" the definite article.

72) **What do we call the words "a" and "an"?** We call the words "a" and "an" the indefinite articles.

73) **What's the difference between "a" and "an"?** The difference between "a" and "an" is that we use "a" before a word that starts with a consonant sound, whereas we use "an" before a word that starts with a vowel sound.

74) **When do we use the indefinite articles "a" and "an"? Give me some examples.** We use the indefinite articles "a" and "an" with singular countable nouns. For example, "a table", "an address".

75) **When do we use the word "one" instead of the indefinite article?** We use the word "one" instead of the indefinite article when we want to emphasize the number.

76) **Give me a sentence with the word "one".** "I like one song on that CD but all the others are really boring".

77) **What are two common uses of the structure "to be" + infinitive with "to"? Give me an example of each.** Two common uses of the structure "to be" + infinitive with "to" are to communicate an arrangement or an obligation. For example, "The two countries are to begin new discussions on trade". "You are to wait until I get back".

78) **When do we use "could" as the past of "can"? Give me an example.** We use "could" as the past of "can" to speak about general abilities. For example, "My grandfather could run very fast when he was a young man".

79) **When don't we use "could" as the past of "can"?** We don't use "could" as the past of "can" if we talk about a particular occasion when somebody managed to do something.

80) **What do we use instead? Give me an example.** We use "was able", "managed" or "succeeded" instead. For example, "The woman gave the children some money, and so they were able to buy some sweets".

81) **What happens when a sentence is negative? Give me an example.** When a sentence is negative, we can use either "couldn't" or "wasn't able". For example, "The woman did not give the children any money, and so they could not buy any sweets".

82) **How do we express the idea of past time with the modals "should" and "ought to"? Give me some examples.** We express the idea of past time with the modals "should" and "ought to" by following them with the word "have" and a past participle. For example, "I should have told her, but I forgot". "They ought to have gone to the police after the accident, but they didn't".

83) **How do we express a future idea with "should" or "ought to"? Give me some examples.** We express a future idea with "should" or "ought to" by using a word or phrase that expresses future time. For example, "She should do it as soon as possible". "They ought to arrive next week".

84) Tell me one common way of making a request. Give me an example.

One common way of making a request is to say "Can you ...?" or "Could you ...?" For example, "Could you possibly lend me your pen for a second, please?"

85) Which is more polite: "can" or "could"?

"Could" is more polite than "can".

86) Tell me another common way of making a request. Give me an example.

Another common way of making a request is to say "Do you mind ...?" or "Would you mind ...?" For example, "Would you mind passing me that book, please?"

87) Would you say "Do you mind …?" or "Would you mind …?" if you wanted to be especially polite?

I would say "Would you mind …?" if I wanted to be especially polite.

88) Give me an example of need as a modal verb in a question.

"Need he come to work next Saturday?"

89) Give me an example of need as a modal verb in a negative sentence.

"She needn't worry about the exam".

90) What does somebody mean if they say that they needn't have done something?

If somebody says that they needn't have done something, it means that they did it, but it was, in fact, not necessary.

91) Can the verb "dare" be used as both an ordinary verb and a modal verb?

Yes, the verb "dare" can be used as both an ordinary verb and a modal verb.

92) What can we say instead of "He doesn't dare to argue with his boss"?

Instead of saying "He doesn't dare to argue with his boss", we can say "He daren't argue with his boss".

93) When we use a noun for the first time in a conversation, do we use the article "a" or "the"? Give me an example.

When we use a noun for the first time in a conversation, we use the article "a". For example, "My uncle has a dog and a cat".

94) **If we then refer to the same thing or person again, do we normally use "a" or "the"? Give me an example.** If we then refer to the same thing or person again, we normally use "the". For example, "My uncle has a cat and a dog. The cat is friendly but I'm afraid of the dog".

95) **In which situation do we use the definite article "the" when we use a noun for the first time? Give me an example.** We use the definite article "the" when we use a noun for the first time only when the speaker and the listener both know who or what is being talked about. For example, "The book which is on the table is yours".

96) **Which of these sentences is correct: "She is a doctor" or "She is doctor"?** "She is a doctor" is correct.

97) **What does it mean if we say we are used to something? Give me an example.** If we say we are used to something, it means that it is not strange or uncomfortable for us anymore because we have experience of it. For example, "He's lived on that busy street for many years, so he is used to the traffic noise".

98) **Why do we put the gerund after the expression "to be used to"? Give me an example.** We put the gerund after the expression "to be used to" because the word "to" is a preposition. For example, "At first it was difficult, but now I'm used to getting up early".

99) **What is the most important use of the definite article "the"? Give me some examples.** The most important use of the definite article "the" is when we are referring to something specific that is known to both the speaker and the listener. For example, "The DVDs I bought yesterday are great"; "Could you close the window, please?"; "The sky's grey today".

100) **How can we sometimes use the word "the" to speak about things in general? Give me an example.** We can sometimes use the word "the" to speak about things in general when we are speaking about <u>types</u> of animals or <u>types</u> of things. For example, "The computer is a very useful thing".

101) When do we put the definite article "the" in front of a name? Give me an example. We put the definite article "the" in front of a name when it is the name of a river, sea, ocean or mountain chain. For example, The Nile, The Andes.

102) When do we put the word "the" in front of the name of a country? Give me an example. We put the word "the" in front of the name of a country only if the name is plural in form. For example, The Netherlands.

103) Tell me the difference between these two sentences: "When she writes the letter, she will drink a coffee" and "When she has written the letter, she will drink a coffee". The difference between these two sentences is that "When she writes the letter, she will drink a coffee" means that it is possible that the two actions will happen at the same time or one after the other, whereas "When she has written the letter, she will drink a coffee" means that she will write first and then, after that, drink.

104) What does the verb "wish" communicate? The verb "wish" communicates the idea that we would like things to be different from the way they in fact are now, or were in the past.

105) What must we remember about the tense of any verb that follows "wish"? Give me an example. We must remember that the tense of any verb that follows "wish" is one step back into the past from the time that we are referring to. For example, "Maria wishes she spoke perfect English".

1   If someone tells you that they would like some coffee, and you would also like some coffee, what can you reply?

2   If someone tells you that they couldn't sleep last night, and you couldn't sleep either, what can you reply?

3   Although sweets aren't good for the health, is it ok to have a bit of chocolate sometimes?

4   What is a snag and give me an example?

5   Do you know which political party suffered defeat in the last elections in your country?

6   What can we say to the other passengers before opening the window of a train or a bus?

7   If a sign above a door says "Mind your head", what does it mean?

8   When parents have to go out together in the evening, who usually minds their baby?

9   What does the idiom "be into something" mean?

10 Is it common in your country for people to eat a cooked breakfast in the morning?

11 Have you determined what you're going to do for your next holidays?

12 For success in life generally, which do you think is more important than anything else: the determination to succeed, luck, hard work, or intelligence?

13 If someone stole a book from a shop and was caught doing so, what'd probably happen?

14 What kind of activities interest you most of all?

15 Supposing a group of foreign students came to stay with you for the weekend, what would you organize for them?

16 What do we mean if we say that someone has a gift for languages?

17 How's steam produced?

18 About how many passengers does the average bus seat?

19 Where's the seat of government in this country?

20 What does the idiom "get on somebody's nerves" mean?

Answers

1 If someone tells me that they would like some coffee, and I would also like some coffee, I can reply "So would I".

2 If someone tells me that they couldn't sleep last night, and I couldn't sleep either, I can reply "Neither could I" or "Nor could I".

3 Yes, although sweets aren't good for the health, it's ok to have a bit of chocolate sometimes.

4 A snag is a small problem; e.g. I need to send him an email but there's just one snag: my Wi-Fi isn't working.

5 Yes, I know which political party suffered defeat in the last elections in my country ~ No, I don't know which political party suffered defeat in the last elections in my country.

6 Before opening the window of a train or a bus, we can say to the other passengers "Excuse me, would you mind if I opened the window?"

7 If a sign above a door says "Mind your head", it means that the door is low and you must be careful not to hit your head on it.

8 When parents have to go out together in the evening, a babysitter usually minds their baby.

9 The idiom "be into something" means have a strong interest in something.

10 Yes, it's common in my country for people to eat a cooked breakfast in the morning. ~ No, it isn't common in my country for people to eat a cooked breakfast in the morning.

11 Yes, I've determined what I'm going to do for my next holidays. ~ No, I haven't determined what I'm going to do for my next holidays.

12 For success in life generally, I think ... is more important than anything else.

13 If someone stole a book from a shop and was caught doing so, the owner of the shop would probably call the police.

14 The kind of activities that interest me most of all are going out with friends, reading etc.

15 Supposing a group of foreign students came to stay with me for the weekend, I'd organize ... for them.

16 If we say that someone has a gift for languages, we mean that they are naturally good at learning languages.

17 Steam is produced by boiling water.

18   The average bus seats about ... passengers.

19   The seat of government in this country is in ...

20   The idiom "get on somebody's nerves" means "irritate somebody".

Revision Exercise 50 (Lessons 104 – 105)

1   Why do we use the words "so" and "not" when replying to something that someone has just said?

2   What are the five senses?

3   Do you prefer bright colours or dark colours?

4   Do you usually feel brighter in the evening than first thing in the morning?

5   Do you spend a great deal of your time doing nothing?

6   Do you think that the personal freedom of the individual is important, or do you think that the individual ought to be made to do the same things and live in the same way as other people?

7   What do we mean by a fierce animal?

8   What had we better do if we want to get high marks in an examination?

9   If you buy clothes and find out later that they don't fit you properly, what do you do?

10   Are you fit to teach English?

11   How would you be able to identify yourself in the street if you were stopped by the police?

12   On what occasions do all the members of a family gather together?

13   What does it mean - "You can't have your cake and eat it"?

14   What do you do when you want to relax?

15   If you could be in the audience at any concert, who would you like to see?

16   What's the most common way to move liquid or gas from one place to another?

17   What's the use of a chimney?

18   What's the difference between the present perfect and the past simple?

19   Why do we say "I ate eggs for breakfast today" and not "I have eaten eggs for breakfast today"?

20 Which of these two sentences is correct: "John got up quite late today" or "John has got up quite late today"?

Answers

1 We use the words "so" and "not" when replying to something that someone has just said to avoid repeating the whole sentence.

2 The five senses are sight, hearing, taste, touch and smell.

3 I prefer ... colours.

4 Yes, I usually feel brighter in the evening than first thing in the morning. ~ No, I don't usually feel brighter in the evening than first thing in the morning; I usually feel more tired.

5 Yes, I spend a great deal of my time doing nothing. ~ No, I don't spend a great deal of my time doing nothing.

6 I think that the personal freedom of the individual is important. ~ I don't think that the personal freedom of the individual is important; I think that the individual ought to be made to do the same things and live in the same way as other people.

7 By a fierce animal we mean a dangerous and wild animal.

8 We had better study hard if we want to get high marks in an examination.

9 If I buy clothes and find out later that they don't fit me properly, I take them back and try to change them.

10 Maybe I'm fit to teach beginner level English.

11 I'd be able to identify myself in the street if I were stopped by the police by showing them my identity card, passport etc.

12 All the members of a family gather together on occasions such as weddings, birthday parties etc.

13 The meaning of "You can't have your cake and eat it" is that sometimes you have to choose between having one thing or another thing, because you cannot have everything you want.

14 When I want to relax, I ...

15 If I could be in the audience at any concert, I'd like to see ...

16 The most common way to move liquid or gas from one place to another is through a pipe.

17   The use of a chimney is to carry the smoke from a fire out of a building and into the air.

18   The difference between the present perfect and the past simple is that we use the present perfect when we are thinking about time before and up to now, whereas we use the past simple when we are thinking about a specific past time.

19   We say "I ate eggs for breakfast today" and not "I have eaten eggs for breakfast today" because we are thinking about what happened at a specific past time - breakfast time. We are not thinking about now.

20   Of those two sentences, "John got up quite late today" is correct.

Revision Exercise 51 (Lessons 106 – 107)

1   Put the word "usually" in this sentence, please: "She can answer his questions".

2   Is oil used a lot in cooking in your country?

3   Do you prefer the heat of the summer rather than the cold of the winter?

4   When you lack sufficient money to buy something, do you wait and save the money or do you buy it on credit?

5   Why do you think it is that some people just don't get on well with their next-door neighbours?

6   Do you think parents should teach their children about the importance of being honest?

7   Do you have more of a taste for plain clothes or for colourful clothes?

8   What kind of work does a plain-clothes policeman do?

9   Do you think life is easier when people speak plainly to each other, that is, speak openly, directly, and honestly to each other?

10   What do you do when you arrive at somebody's house to pay a visit?

11   If someone rang you while you were busy talking to another person, would you answer the call?

12   Have you ever rung someone up without realizing how late it was and accidentally woken them up?

13   What do we do when we change a question from direct into indirect speech?

14 What do we do when we change an imperative from direct into indirect speech?

15 With negative imperatives, what do we do?

16 What do we do when we change a request from direct into indirect speech?

17 What, generally speaking, is the difference between the words "house" and "home"?

18 Do you think it's a good thing for boys and girls to leave home when they are teenagers?

19 What's the difference between housework and homework?

20 What does the idiom "I couldn't care less" mean?

Answers

1 She can usually answer his questions.

2 Yes, oil's used a lot in cooking in my country. ~ No, oil isn't used a lot in cooking in my country.

3 Yes, I prefer the heat of the summer rather than the cold of the winter. ~ No, I don't prefer the heat of the summer rather than the cold of the winter.

4 When I lack sufficient money to buy something, I wait and save the money/I buy it on credit.

5 I think the reason that some people just don't get on well with their next-door neighbours is that we can choose our friends, but cannot choose our neighbours.

6 Yes, I think parents should teach their children about the importance of being honest.

7 I have more of a taste for plain/colourful clothes.

8 A plain-clothes policeman does detective work, the kind of work a policeman in uniform could not do because he would be too noticeable.

9 Yes, I think life is easier when people speak plainly to each other, that is, speak openly, directly, and honestly to each other. ~ No, I don't think life is easier when people speak plainly to each other, that is, speak openly, directly, and honestly to each other.

10 When I arrive at somebody's house to pay a visit, I ring the doorbell.

11 Yes, if someone rang me while I was busy talking to another person, I'd answer the call. ~ No, if someone rang me while I was busy talking to another person, I wouldn't answer the call.

12 Yes, I've rung someone up without realizing how late it was and accidentally woken them up. ~ No, I've never rung someone up without realizing how late it was and accidentally woken them up.

13 When we change a question from direct into indirect speech, we move the verb one step back into the past, we use "asked" instead of "said", and we do not use the question form or a question mark.

14 When we change an imperative from direct into indirect speech, we use "told", "commanded" or "ordered", and we use the infinitive without "to" instead of the imperative.

15 With negative imperatives, we put "not" before the infinitive.

16 When we change a request from direct into indirect speech, we use "asked", and we can use the same constructions that we use for indirect questions or imperatives.

17 Generally speaking, the difference between the words "house" and "home" is that we use "house" when we are thinking about a physical building, whereas we use "home" in a more abstract sense to mean the place where we live or come from.

18 Yes, I think it's a good thing for boys and girls to leave home when they are teenagers. ~ No, I don't think it's a good thing for boys and girls to leave home when they are teenagers.

19 The difference between housework and homework is that housework is the work we have to do in the house, such as the washing, cleaning, washing up etc., whereas homework is the work a pupil has to do at home.

20 The idiom "I couldn't care less" means "it is of no interest or importance to me".

Revision Exercise 52 (Lessons 108 – 109)

1 What's the difference between "He hardly works" and "He works hard"?

2 If you had a car accident but your car was hardly damaged, would you get it repaired or would you just leave it?

3 What kind of jobs make great demands on one's nerves?

4 Do you think human life could continue if there was a nuclear war?

5 What do we mean by a pair of earrings?

6 Can a bird fly with only one wing?

7   Do you have any original paintings hanging up on the walls of your home?

8   Can we use future verb forms in time clauses and conditional clauses?

9   What's the difference between a "racehorse", a "horse race" and a "racecourse"?

10 Do you think the human race will always go on living?

11 Do you agree it's dangerous for a young child to cross the road unless they have an adult with them?

12 If you were walking across a park and a ball rolled your way, would you kick it back to its owner or would you pick it up and throw it back?

13 What's the difference between a teacup and a cup of tea?

14 In the animal world, which is usually more colourful: the male or the female?

15 Which would you say was more profitable in business: to deal in cars or to deal in food?

16 What do we mean when we say we make a deal with someone?

17 Do you think you could run a large factory, or don't you think you could even run a small coffee shop?

18 What words can we use when we want to emphasize the person who does the action in a particular sentence?

19 Does someone else usually make breakfast for you or do you make it yourself?

20 What's the difference between these two sentences: "He painted the house himself" and "He painted the house by himself"?

Answers

1   The difference between "He hardly works" and "He works hard" is that "He hardly works" means that he does almost no work, whereas "He works hard" means that he works a lot.

2   If I had a car accident but my car was hardly damaged, I'd get it repaired/ just leave it.

3   The kind of jobs that make great demands on one's nerves are police officer, bus driver, teacher, and any kind of job where one has to work with the public.

4   Yes, I think human life could continue if there was a nuclear war. ~ No, I don't think human life could continue if there was a nuclear war.

5   By a pair of earrings, we mean two earrings that are the same.

6   No, a bird can't fly with only one wing; it must have a pair of wings.

7   Yes, I have some original paintings hanging up on the walls of my home. ~ No, I don't have any original paintings hanging up on the walls of my home.

8   No, we can't use future verb forms in time clauses and conditional clauses.

9   The difference between a "racehorse", a "horse race" and a "racecourse" is that a "racehorse" is a horse we use for racing, a "horse race" is a race between horses, and a "racecourse" is a place where people meet in order to race horses.

10 Yes, I think the human race will always go on living. ~ No, I don't think the human race will always go on living.

11 Yes, I agree it's dangerous for a young child to cross the road unless they have an adult with them.

12 If I were walking across a park and a ball rolled my way, I'd kick it back to its owner/pick it up and throw it back.

13 The difference between a teacup and a cup of tea is that a teacup is a cup for tea, whereas a cup of tea is a cup with tea in it.

14 In the animal world, the male is usually more colourful than the female.

15 I'd say that it was more profitable in business to deal in cars/to deal in food.

16 When we say we make a deal with someone we mean we agree to give someone something in return for something they will give us, or to do something for someone in return for something they will do for us.

17 I think I could run a large factory. ~ I don't think I could run a large factory or even run a small coffee shop.

18 When we want to emphasize the person who does the action in a particular sentence, we can use "myself", "yourself", "himself" etc.

19 Someone else usually makes breakfast for me. ~ I usually make breakfast myself.

20 The difference between these two sentences is that the first sentence emphasizes the fact that "he" painted the house not someone else, whereas the second sentence means he painted the house alone, without any help.

Revision Exercise 53 (Lessons 110 – 111)

1   Are there any mountains in your country where snow settles on the top even in the middle of summer?

2   Would you find it difficult to settle in a foreign country forever?

3   What does a teacher say to pupils when they are making too much noise?

4   Would you say that success in life was partly a question of luck?

5   Is it often difficult for parents to get their children to tidy their rooms?

6   Would you be afraid to act on the stage?

7   At what stage of your English studies are you at the moment: beginner, intermediate or advanced?

8   If you followed a river upstream, where would it eventually lead you to?

9   If you saw a stream of people streaming out of a building in a hurry, what'd you think?

10 How is a non-defining clause separated from the main part of the sentence?

11 What happens to the branch of a tree when it waves too much in the wind?

12 What do you recommend that people do in order to succeed in life?

13 What, generally speaking, is the difference between an injury and a wound?

14 Do you think children ought to be made to study, or do you think studying ought to be voluntary?

15 If we don't know the name of the person we're writing to, how do we begin a formal letter or email?

16 How do we generally end such a letter or email?

17 If you order goods online but they don't arrive, can you cancel the order and get a refund?

18 Why do people go on strike?

19 What does a manager do?

20 Which do you think it's better to possess: brains, beauty or money?

Answers

1   Yes, there are some mountains in my country where snow settles on the top even in the middle of summer. ~ No, there aren't any mountains in my country where snow settles on the top even in the middle of summer.

2   Yes, I'd find it difficult to settle in a foreign country forever. ~ No, I wouldn't find it difficult to settle in a foreign country forever.

3   A teacher says "Come on now, settle down" to pupils when they are making too much noise.

4   Yes, I'd say that success in life was partly a question of luck. ~ No, I wouldn't say that success in life was partly a question of luck.

5   Yes, it's often difficult for parents to get their children to tidy their rooms.

6   Yes, I'd be afraid to act on the stage. ~ No, I wouldn't be afraid to act on the stage.

7   I'm at an intermediate stage of my English studies at the moment.

8   If you followed a river upstream, it'd eventually lead you to the mountains or hills.

9   If I saw a stream of people streaming out of a building in a hurry, I'd think that either the building was on fire or that the people had just finished work.

10   A non-defining clause is separated from the main part of the sentence by commas.

11   When the branch of a tree waves too much in the wind, it breaks and falls to the ground.

12   I recommend that people ... in order to succeed in life.

13   Generally speaking, the difference between an injury and a wound is that we use we use the word "injury" for something we receive by accident and "wound" for something we receive from fighting.

14   I think children ought to be made to study. ~ I don't think children ought to be made to study; I think studying ought to be voluntary.

15   If we don't know the name of the person we're writing to, we begin a formal letter or email with the words "Dear Sir" or "Dear Madam".

16   We generally end such a letter or email with the words "Yours faithfully" or "Kind regards" or "Best regards".

17   Yes, if I order goods online but they don't arrive, I can cancel the order and get a refund.

18   People go on strike because they want more money or better working conditions.

19   A manager manages a business, or part of a business; that is, he makes important decisions about how the business operates.

20   I think it's better to possess brains/beauty/money.

1   When children play together, do they often pretend to be adults?

2   If you write the address on an envelope but leave out the postcode, will the letter still arrive?

3   Would you find it difficult to behave naturally if you met someone really famous?

4   If you thought one of your workmates was stealing money from the company you worked for, what would you do?

5   What kind of things do you look forward to most?

6   If you were the owner of a business and one of your workers stole something from the business, would you give them a second chance, or would you dismiss them at once?

7   Many years ago, did humans have to hunt animals for food?

8   What do we use a pair of scissors for?

9   What does the idiom "let yourself go" mean?

10 If you were in a bus going downhill and the driver suddenly lost control of the bus, what'd you do?

11 Why don't trains always arrive when they are due?

12 If a friend of yours is wearing clothes that look totally wrong on them, do you tell them?

13 Why do housemates sometimes argue with one another?

14 Can a dentist do anything about irregular teeth?

15 What's the difference between "dust" and "powder"?

16 What do you consider to be a good cause worth collecting money for?

17 If you rang somebody up when they were at work but they weren't available immediately, would you wait, leave a message or call back later?

18 What artificial parts of the body can science provide us with?

19 What does the idiom "pull someone's leg" mean?

20 What do we mean by the "rush hour" in a large city?

Answers

1 Yes, when children play together, they often pretend to be adults.

2 Yes, if you write the address on an envelope but leave out the postcode, the letter will still arrive, but it may take longer.

3 Yes, I'd find it difficult to behave naturally if I met someone really famous. ~ No, I wouldn't find it difficult to behave naturally if I met someone really famous.

4 If I thought one of my workmates was stealing money from the company I worked for, I'd ...

5 The kind of things I look forward to most are ...

6 If I were the owner of a business and one of my workers stole something from the business, I'd give them a second chance/dismiss them at once.

7 Yes, many years ago, humans had to hunt animals for food.

8 We use a pair of scissors for cutting paper etc.

9 The idiom "let yourself go" means "relax and enjoy yourself".

10 If I were in a bus going downhill and the driver suddenly lost control of the bus, I'd try to take control of the bus etc.

11 Trains don't always arrive when they are due because of bad weather, breakdowns etc.

12 Yes, if a friend of mine is wearing clothes that look totally wrong on them, I tell them. ~ No, if a friend of mine is wearing clothes that look totally wrong on them, I don't tell them.

13 Housemates sometimes argue with one another because ...

14 Yes, a dentist can do something about irregular teeth.

15 The difference between dust and powder is that "dust" is natural and collects on objects, whereas "powder" is something that is made.

16 I consider ... to be a good cause worth collecting money for.

17 If I rang somebody up when they were at work but they weren't available immediately, I'd wait/leave a message/call back later.

18 Science can provide us with artificial arms, legs, teeth, hair etc.

19 The idiom "pull someone's leg" means "joke with someone, by making them believe something that is not true".

20 By the "rush hour" in a large city, we mean the time when everyone rushes to work or home from work.

Revision Exercise 55 (Lessons 114 – 115)

1   What's the difference between a dish and a plate?

2   Are you for or against the police carrying arms when they're walking around the streets on duty?

3   What do members of the general public do when they see a criminal seize a woman's handbag in the street?

4   What's the difference between "wage" and "salary"?

5   What kind of people don't earn a steady wage or salary?

6   How do we generally form the plural of a noun ending in "f" or "fe"?

7   Where do deer prefer to live: in woods or open fields?

8   What kind of things do people often mention when they're telling you about a holiday they've just been on?

9   If a friend buys you a drink in a bar, do you normally insist on giving them the money or do you just buy them a drink the next time?

10 If you stayed at a hotel on holiday, would you choose "full board", "half board" or "bed and breakfast"?

11 Do you know when your local football team play their next game?

12 Do you keep an account of all the money you spend?

13 What sometimes happens if two people differ greatly in their opinions on a particular subject?

14 Have you ever had private English lessons?

15 When you were a child, did you always like what you were given for your birthday?

16 When do some people prefer to use the relative pronoun "whom" instead of "who"?

17 In normal spoken English, what do we say instead of "We need to contact the customer from whom she took the payment"?

18 Do you know the people whose house is next to yours?

19 Have you ever been searched at an airport?

20 Do you support any particular football team?

Answers

1   The difference between a dish and a plate is that a plate is flat, whereas a dish is deeper. We usually eat food from a plate, whereas we serve food from a dish.

2   I'm for the police carrying arms when they're walking around the streets on duty. ~ I'm against the police carrying arms when they're walking around the streets on duty.

3   When members of the general public see a criminal seize a woman's handbag in the street, some run after the criminal or shout for help, but most people just stand and look too surprised to do anything.

4   The difference between "wage" and "salary" is that we generally use the word "wage" for a non-professional job, or a job in which a person earns a fixed amount of money for each hour they work, whereas we generally use "salary" for a professional job, or a job in which a person earns a fixed amount of money each year.

5   The kind of people who don't earn a steady wage or salary are actors, artists, writers etc.

6   We generally form the plural of a noun ending in "f" or "fe" by changing the "f" or "fe" to "ves".

7   Deer prefer to live in woods.

8   People often mention the weather, food etc. when they're telling you about a holiday they've just been on.

9   If a friend buys me a drink in a bar, I normally insist on giving them the money/ don't normally insist on giving them the money; I just buy them a drink the next time.

10   If I stayed at a hotel on holiday, I'd choose "full board"/"half board"/"bed and breakfast".

11   Yes, I know when my local football team play their next game. ~ No, I don't know when my local football team play their next game.

12   Yes, I keep an account of all the money I spend. ~ No, I don't keep an account of all the money I spend.

13   If two people differ greatly in their opinions on a particular subject, they sometimes have an argument.

14   Yes, I've had private English lessons. ~ No, I've never had private English lessons.

15   Yes, when I was a child, I always liked what I was given for my birthday. ~ No, when I was a child, I didn't always like what I was given for my birthday.

16   Some people prefer to use the relative pronoun "whom" instead of "who" with formal English, when the relative pronoun is not the subject of the verb that follows.

17   In normal spoken English, instead of "We need to contact the customer from whom she took the payment", we say "We need to contact the customer who she took the payment from".

18   Yes, I know the people whose house is next to mine. ~ No, I don't know the people whose house is next to mine.

19   Yes, I've been searched at an airport. ~ No, I've never been searched at an airport.

20   Yes, I support a particular football team. ~ No, I don't support any particular football team.

Revision Exercise 56 (Lessons 116 – 117)

1   If you were caught red-handed stealing something, would you declare yourself innocent before the judge when you appeared in court for your trial?

2   In writing, what do we mean by upper case and lower case letters?

3   If you were a great person, what kind of monument would you like the public to raise in your honour after you were dead?

4   What's the difference between a transitive verb and an intransitive verb?

5   What is scorn?

6   How does a cowboy keep his cattle together?

7   What happens at harvest time?

8   Where do we find railings?

9   What's the meaning of the idiom "to be on about"?

10   Name some English nouns that are never used in the plural, please.

11   What do you think is the best piece of advice a father can give to his son?

12   What would you say were the advantages of mass-production?

13   When a boy and a girl have a date, is it more common for the boy to pick the girl up at her house or to meet her somewhere in town?

14 What's the difference between a drum and a barrel?

15 What's the difference between the words "harbour" and "port"?

16 What has been the most important event of your life so far?

17 Are you the kind of person who likes to put his nose into things that don't concern him?

18 If you won the lottery, how would you celebrate?

19 If you're planning to travel around the world, is it essential to have an up-to-date passport?

20 What does the idiom "a piece of cake" mean?

Answers

1 Yes, if I were caught red-handed stealing something, I'd declare myself innocent before the judge when I appeared in court for my trial. ~ No, if I were caught red-handed stealing something, I wouldn't declare myself innocent before the judge when I appeared in court for my trial.

2 In writing, by upper case and lower case letters we mean capital letters and small letters.

3 If I were a great person, the kind of monument I'd like the public to raise in my honour after I were dead would be a statue etc.

4 The difference between a transitive verb and an intransitive verb is that a transitive verb has an object, whereas an intransitive verb does not have an object.

5 Scorn is a feeling that somebody or something is not worthy of our respect.

6 A cowboy keeps his cattle together by constantly riding around them on a horse or motorbike.

7 Farmers gather their crops at harvest time.

8 We find railings on a balcony to stop people falling, or sometimes around a piece of private land to stop people entering.

9 The meaning of the idiom "to be on about" is "to mean".

10 Some English nouns that are never used in the plural are "advice", "furniture", "information", "knowledge", "progress" and "news".

11 I think the best piece of advice a father can give to his son is ...

12 I'd say the advantages of mass-production were that products can be made quickly and more cheaply.

13   When a boy and a girl have a date, it's more common for the boy to pick the girl up at her house/to meet her somewhere in town.

14   The difference between a drum and a barrel is that a drum is usually made of metal and has straight sides, whereas a barrel is usually made of wood and has round sides.

15   The difference between the words "harbour" and "port" is that a harbour is anywhere a boat or ship is protected from the weather, whereas a port is a place where goods are put onto or taken off a ship, or where passengers board a ship.

16   The most important event of my life so far has been …

17   Yes, I'm the kind of person who likes to put his nose into things that don't concern him. ~ No, I'm not the kind of person who likes to put his nose into things that don't concern him.

18   If I won the lottery, I'd celebrate by …

19   Yes, if you're planning to travel around the world, it's essential to have an up-to-date passport.

20   The idiom "a piece of cake" means "extremely easy to do".

INDEX

Index

STAGE 8
VOCABULARY

Arabic Vocabulary

LESSON 112

603	joke	يمزح/نكتة
603	pretend	يتظاهر
603	envelope	مظروف
603	stamp	طابع بريدي
603	leave out	يحذف
603	postcode	الرمز البريدي
604	naturally	بشكل طبيعي
604	recent	أخير
604	so-so	متوسط
604	mate	رفيق
604	housemate	شريك البيت
604	flatmate	شريك الشقة
604	classmate	زميل الدراسة
604	workmate	زميل العمل
605	to look forward to	يتطلع إلى
605	let me see	دعني أفكر
606	chance	الفرصة
606	dismiss	فصل من الخدمة
606	jungle	الأدغال
606	fifty-fifty	مناصفة
606	take a chance	يغامر
606	whistle	يصفر
606	hunt	يصطاد
607	deed	صنيع
607	grease	تشحيم
607	scissors	المقص
607	take control	يسيطر
607	lose control	يفقد السيطرة
607	due	المستحق دفعه/متوقع
607	due to	بسبب
608	grandmother	جدة
608	grandfather	الجد
608	great-grandmother	أم الجدة
608	great-grandfather	أبو الجد
608	mostly	غالبًا
608	totally	تمامًا
609	sentence	الجملة

LESSON 113

610	discuss	يناقش
610	discussion	المناقشة
610	argue	يجادل
610	argument	جدال
610	quarrel	يتشاجر
610	anger	الغضب
610	reason	يناقش منطقيا
611	regular	المنتظم/عادي
611	do something about	افعل شيئًا بخصوص
611	blow up	يفجر
612	dust	الغبار
612	powder	المسحوق
612	collect	يجمع
612	face powder	مساحيق الوجه
612	meeting	الاجتماع
612	football match	مباراة كرة القدم
612	Red Cross	الصليب الأحمر
613	furniture	الأثاث
613	furnish	يؤثث
613	available	متاح
613	human being	إنسان

613	artificial	صناعي
614	kiss	يقبل
614	rush	تزاحم/يزاحم
614	hero	البطل

LESSON 114

616	dish	الصحن
616	serve	يقدم
616	to be for (or against) something	أن تؤيد (أو تعترض) على شيء ما
616	arms	أسلحة
616	fox	الثعلب
616	fox hunting	صيد الثعالب
617	seize	يستولي على
617	handbag	حقيبة اليد
617	break out	يندلع
617	wage	الأجر
617	salary	الراتب
617	payment	دفعة
617	profession	المهنة
617	non - professional	غير مهني
617	steady	ثابت
617	seasonal	موسمي
617	seaside	شاطئ البحر
617	painter	الرسام
617	pianist	عازف البيانو
617	surgeon	الجراح
618	leaf	ورقة الشجر
618	loaf	رغيف الخبز
618	shelf	الرف
618	cliff	جرف
618	deer	الغزال
618	wood	الخشب
619	mention	يذكر
619	tell off	يوبخ
619	partner	الشريك
619	insist	يصر
620	board	اللوح
620	floorboard	ألواح الأرضية
620	noticeboard	لوحة الإعلانات
620	blackboard	السبورة
620	deck	ظهر المركب
620	port	ميناء
620	director	مدير

LESSON 115

622	timetable	جدول زمني
622	schedule	جدول
622	account	بيان/سرد قصة/حساب
623	greedy	طماع
623	satisfied	راض
623	crop	المحصول
623	differ	يختلف
623	private	خاص
624	what	ما
624	whom	الذي
626	whose	الذي له
626	search	يبحث/يفتش
626	support	يدعم/يشجع
627	religious	متدين

LESSON 116

628	declare	يعلن
628	red-handed	متلبس بالجريمة
628	innocent	البريء
628	upper	العليا/الكبير
628	middle	الوسطى
628	working	العاملة
628	class	الطبقة
628	society	المجتمع
628	aristocracy	الأرستقراطية
628	industrialist	من أرباب الصناعة
628	case	الحرف
628	lower	الصغير
629	raise	يرفع/ينشئ/ينصب
629	to be excused	أن يعذر
629	monument	نصب تذكاري
629	honour	الشرف
629	statue	التمثال
630	transitive	الفعل المتعدي
631	respect	الاحترام
631	scorn	يحتقر
631	worthy	يستحق
631	term	فصل مدرسي
631	worship	يتعبد
632	cattle	الماشية
632	cowboy	راعي البقر
632	harvest	حصاد
632	mother-in-law	الحماة
632	father-in-law	الحمو
632	rail	قضيب
632	railing	حاجز حديدي/قضيب السكة الحديدية
632	run	يركض
632	protection	حماية
632	balcony	شرفة

LESSON 117

634	knowledge	المعرفة/العلم
634	progress	تقدم
634	item	بند/شيء
634	encyclopedia	الموسوعة
635	mass	جمع/بالجملة
635	advantage	ميزة
635	disadvantage	عيب
635	mass – production	الإنتاج بالجملة
635	production	الإنتاج
635	product	منتج
635	identical	متطابق
635	quality	نوعية
636	pick up	يلتقط/يأخذ
636	date	يخرج مع ١ موعد
636	vocabulary	المفردات
636	prevent	يمنع
636	drum	يقرع/يطبل/طبلة، جالون حديد
636	harbour	المرفأ
636	port	ميناء
637	nosey	فضولي
637	masculine	المذكر
637	feminine	المؤنث
637	god	إله
637	goddess	آلهة
637	prince	أمير
637	princess	أميرة
638	nephew	ابن الأخ أو الأخت
638	niece	بنت الأخ أو الأخت
638	landlord	مالك العقار
638	landlady	مالكة العقار
638	widower	أرمل
638	widow	أرملة

638	event	حدث
638	eventful	حافل بالأحداث
638	uneventful	خالي من الأحداث
638	concern	يعنى بـ
639	celebrate	يحتفل
639	celebration	الاحتفال
639	New Year's Eve	عشية رأس السنة الجديدة
639	up to date	حديث
639	out of date	قديم/ منتهي الصلاحية
639	essential	ضروري

LESSON 118

640	article	أداة
641	countable	قابل للعد
641	uncountable	غير قابل للعد
642	worm	الدودة
642	silkworm	دودة القز
642	silk	الحرير
642	limb	الأطراف
642	poison	سم
643	cave	الكهف
643	bat	الخفاش
643	deserve	يستحق
643	frequent (verb)	(يتردد (فعل
643	frequent (adjective)	(متكرر (صفة
643	frequently (adverb)	(تكرارا (ظرف
644	attract	يجذب
644	attention	انتباه
644	attraction	جذاب
644	attractive	جذاب
644	good-looking	حسن المظهر
644	the rest	البقية
644	miserable	بائس
645	emotion	العاطفة
645	emotional	انفعالي

LESSON 119

646	firstly	أولاً
646	secondly	ثانيًا
646	head teacher	الناظر
646	study	مكتب
647	vote	يصوت
647	nurse	يعتني بـ
647	nursery	الحضانة
647	unemployment	البطالة
647	take off	يقلع
647	land	يهبط
647	seat belt	حزام المقعد
648	practice	عمليا/ممارسة
648	theory	النظرية
648	practical	عملي
648	take into account	يأخذ في الحسبان
648	set up	يؤسس
649	nature	الطبيعة
649	human nature	الطبيعة البشرية
650	compete	يتنافس
650	competition	المنافسة
650	energy	الطاقة
650	efficient	فعال
650	suit	يناسب
650	suitable	مناسب
651	effect	أثر
651	perfect	تام
651	to go up to	يذهب إلى
651	sunshine	ضياء الشمس

LESSON 120

653	polish	يلمع
653	ability	القدرة

Arabic vocabulary

Chinese Vocabulary

Chinese vocabulary

683 axe...斧子
683 equally ....平等地

LESSON 125

684 Alps ....阿尔卑斯山
684 Andes ....安第斯山
684 Himalayas...........................喜马拉雅山
684 Netherlands...........................荷兰
685 present (noun +adj)....................礼物；现在的
685 present (verb)..........................出席；赠与；呈现
686 swear - swore - sworn 说脏话（过去式swore；过去分词sworn)
687 lazy ....懒惰的
687 idle.................无所事事的；不工作的
687 play...................................戏剧
687 scene................................场景
688 verse................................诗句
688 chorus.............................重唱部分
688 pray ....祈祷
688 prayer ....祈祷者
688 combine ....结合
689 heads.............................正面朝上的
689 tails.............................（硬币）背面

LESSON 126

690 extend...................延伸；伸出，伸展
690 as far as ....远到
691 trust ....信任；信托
691 dependent ....依赖的
691 independent...........................独立的
692 punctual...........................准时的
692 row.................................划船
692 oar ....桨
692 wish ....希望
693 ideal.................................理想
693 theoretical............................理论的
693 actual.............................实际的
693 actually ....实际上
694 check ....检查
694 change...............................零钱
694 log.................................木料
694 fireplace..............................壁炉
694 common sense........................常识
695 tool.................................工具
695 bean ....豆

Czech Vocabulary

LESSON 112

603 joke......................................žert/vtip/žertovat
603 pretend ....předstírat
603 envelope.................................... obálka
603 stamp....................................... známka
603 leave out.....................................vynechat
603 postcode...................... poštovní směrovací číslo
604 naturally........................... přirozeně/samozřejmě
604 recent .... nedávný
604 so-so......................................průměrný
604 mate ....kamarád
604 housemate......................... spolubydlící v domě
604 flatmate................... spolubydlící v bytě
604 classmate ....spolužák
604 workmate................................spolupracovník
605 to look forward to............................těšit se na
605 let me see..................................moment prosím
606 chance...................................... šance
606 dismiss .... propustit
606 jungle .... džungle
606 fifty-fifty ....padesát ku padesáti/nerozhodný
606 take a chance .... chopit se příležitosti
606 whistle .... pískat
606 hunt ....lovit
607 deed .... čin
607 grease .... mazadlo
607 scissors ....nůžky
607 take control................................. převzít kontrolu
607 lose control .... ztratit kontrolu
607 due .... splatný/mít povinnost/v termínu
607 due to .... v důsledku/z důvodu
608 grandmother.............................babička
608 grandfather............................... dědeček
608 great-grandmother......................... prababička
608 great-grandfather........................... pradědeček
608 mostly...................................většinou
608 totally.. úplně
609 sentence.................................... věta

LESSON 113

610 discuss .... hovořit/projednat
610 discussion...............................diskuse
610 argue ....hádat se/zdůvodnit
610 argument .... hádka
610 quarrel .... roztržka/přít se
610 anger .... hněv
610 reason ....důvod/zdůvodnit
611 regular ....pravidelný
611 do something about................něco s tím udělat
611 blow up....................... vyhodit do vzduchu
612 dust..prach
612 powder......................................prášek
612 collect .... sbírat/shromáždit
612 face powder.................................obličejový pudr
612 meeting........................... setkání/porada
612 football match ....fotbalový zápas
612 Red Cross ....Červený kříž
613 furniture .... nábytek
613 furnish................................ zařídit si/vybavit
613 available ....k dispozici/dostupný
613 human being................................. lidská bytost
613 artificial .... umělý

614 kiss ....polibek/políbit
614 rush .... spěchat
614 hero ....hrdina

LESSON 114

616 dish.. mělká miska/jídlo
616 serve...................................... podávat/servírovat
616 to be for (or against) somethings něčím souhlasit či nesouhlasit
616 arms ....zbraně
616 fox..liška
616 fox hunting.............................hon na lišku
617 seize....................................... zmocnit se/uloupit
617 handbag ....kabelka
617 break out ....vypuknout (válka)
617 wage....................................... mzda
617 salary.. plat
617 payment.............................platba/výplata
617 profession...................................profese
617 non - professional...................... neprofesionální
617 steady..................................pevný/stálý
617 seasonal .... sezónní
617 seaside .... přímořský
617 painter ....malíř
617 pianist ....klavírista
617 surgeon ....chirurg
618 leaf...list
618 loaf..................................... bochník
618 shelf...police
618 cliff .... útes
618 deer .... jelen
618 wood .... les
619 mention ....zmínit se/uvést
619 tell off.. vynadat
619 partner ....partner
619 insist .... trvat na
620 board ...deska/nalodit se/představenstvo/strava a ubytování
620 floorboard ....podlahová deska
620 noticeboard........................... informační tabule
620 blackboard.......................................školní tabule
620 deck .... paluba
620 port .... přístav
620 director ....ředitel

LESSON 115

622 timetable......................jízdní řád/harmonogram
622 schedule...................................rozvrh
622 account.............................. popis/účet/evidence
623 greedy ....chamtivý
623 satisfied ....spokojený
623 crop .... plodina
623 differ ....lišit se
623 private.................................. soukromý
624 what... co
624 whom.................................komu/jemuž
626 whose.................................čí/jehož
626 search.......................................hledat
626 support ....podpírat/podporovat
627 religious ....náboženský

Czech vocabulary

LESSON 116

628	declare	prohlásit
628	red-handed	při činu
628	innocent	nevinen
628	upper	horní
628	middle	střední
628	working	pracující
628	class	třída
628	society	společenství
628	aristocracy	aristokracie
628	industrialist	průmyslník
628	case	(velká a malá písmena)
628	lower	dolní
629	raise	zvednout/vztyčit/vychovávat
629	to be excused	být omluven
629	monument	pomník/památník
629	honour	čest
629	statue	socha
630	transitive	přechodný
631	respect	respekt
631	scorn	pohrdání
631	worthy	být hoden/stát za to
631	term	semestr
631	worship	uctívat
632	cattle	dobytek
632	cowboy	pastevec
632	harvest	žně
632	mother-in-law	tchýně
632	father-in-law	tchán
632	rail	kolej
632	railing	zábradlí
632	run	provozovat/jet
632	protection	ochrana
632	balcony	balkon

LESSON 117

634	knowledge	znalosti
634	progress	pokrok
634	item	položka/kus
634	encyclopedia	encyklopedie
635	mass	masa/masový
635	advantage	výhoda
635	disadvantage	nevýhoda
635	mass – production	masová výroba
635	production	výroba
635	product	výrobek
635	identical	totožný
635	quality	kvalita
635	pick up	zvednout/vyzvednout/pochytit
635	date	schůzka
635	vocabulary	slovník
636	prevent	zabránit/předejít
636	drum	bubnovat/buben
636	harbour	přístav
636	port	přístav (město)
637	nosey	všetečný/zvědavý
637	masculine	mužský (rod)
637	feminine	ženský (rod)
637	god	bůh
637	goddess	bohyně
637	prince	princ
637	princess	princezna
638	nephew	synovec
638	niece	neteř
638	landlord	majitel domu
638	landlady	majitelka domu
638	widower	vdovec
638	widow	vdova

638	event	událost
638	eventful	plný událostí
638	uneventful	jednotvárný
638	concern	týkat se
639	celebrate	slavit
639	celebration	oslava
639	New Year's Eve	Silvestr
639	up to date	moderní/nejnovější
639	out of date	nemoderní/prošlý
639	essential	nezbytný

LESSON 118

640	article	člen
641	countable	počitatelný
641	uncountable	nepočitatelný
642	worm	červ
642	silkworm	bourec morušový
642	silk	hedvábí
642	limb	končetina
642	poison	jed
643	cave	jeskyně
643	bat	netopýr
643	deserve	zasloužit
643	frequent (verb)	navštěvovat
643	frequent (adjective)	častý
643	frequently (adverb)	často
644	attract	přivábit
644	attention	atrakce
644	attraction	atraktivní
644	attractive	pozornost
644	good-looking	přitažlivý
644	the rest	zbytek
644	miserable	mizerný/chudý
645	emotion	emoce
645	emotional	dojatý

LESSON 119

646	firstly	za prvé
646	secondly	za druhé
646	head teacher	ředitel školy
646	study	kabinet
647	vote	volit
647	nurse	opatrovat/pečovat o
647	nursery	jesle/školka
647	unemployment	nezaměstnanost
647	take off	vzlétnout
647	land	přistát
647	seat belt	bezpečnostní pás
648	practice	praxe
648	theory	teorie
648	practical	praktický
648	take into account	vzít v úvahu
648	set up	založit
649	nature	povaha
649	human nature	lidská povaha
650	compete	soutěžit
650	competition	soutěž
650	energy	energie
650	efficient	účinný/efektivní
650	suit	slušet/hodit se
650	suitable	vhodný
651	effect	účinek/vliv/dopad
651	perfect	naprostý
651	to go up to	přistoupit k
651	sunshine	sluneční paprsky

LESSON 120

653	polish	leštit
653	ability	schopnost

653 expense..výdaj
653 postpone...odložit
654 stress.. stres
654 stressful..stresující
654 afterwards..poté
654 first of all .... především
654 attend ....navštěvovat/obsluhovat/dávat pozor
654 shopkeeper.................................majitel prodejny
655 move.. pohnout/dojmout
655 tear ....slza
655 pass...podat
656 spoil - spoilt - spoilt...... zkazit/rozmazlit: přítomný
čas - minulý čas - příčestí minulé
656 discipline.. kázeň
656 hunger .... hlad
656 share ....sdílet/podíl

LESSON 121

659 association ....asociace/sdružení
659 automobile.......................................automobilový
659 disturb...rušit
659 concentrate...................................soustředit se
659 courage .... odvaha
659 virtue .... ctnost
660 loyal.. oddaný
660 loyalty .... oddanost
660 companion.......................................společník
660 spirit............... nadšení/duch/nálada/duše/destilát
660 spiritual.. duchovní
660 evil...zlý
661 flow...téci/plynout
661 festival ....festival
661 feast.. hostina
661 dare ....odvážit se
661 challenge...výzva
662 bring up ....vychovat
662 solve ....řešit
662 calculator .... kalkulačka
663 fix.........................upevnit/naplánovat/připevnit
663 hammer..kladivo
663 nail..hřebík
663 fingernail...nehet
663 criticize ....kritizovat

LESSON 122

665 yard ....dvůr
665 courtyard ....nádvoří
665 enclose..obehnat
665 space..prostor
665 amuse..bavit se
665 comic..komický
665 pass (the time)....................... plynout/ubíhat
665 cards.. karty
665 waiting room............................. čekárna
665 amusement.. zábava
666 hobby...koníček
666 photography ....fotografování
666 order..pořadí
666 pack.. balit
666 packed......................................zaplněný/narvaný
666 suitcase ....kufr
666 shorts ....kraťasy
666 T-shirt .... tričko
667 thorn ....trn
667 rose ....růže
667 afford ....dovolit si
667 agreement ....dohoda
667 basket...košík
667 trolley...vozík

667 nut ....ořech
668 regarding .... ohledně
668 material...materiál
668 duvet..peřina
668 cotton.. bavlna
668 leather .... kůže
668 convenience .... vymoženost/výhoda/pohodlí
668 convenient.................................... vyhovující
668 inconvenient .... nepohodlí
668 inconvenience ....nevyhovující
668 dining room...................................... jídelna
668 sensitive .... citlivý
668 offend ....urazit
668 criticism ....kritika
668 thermometer...................................teploměr
669 sensible ....praktický
669 reasonable.. rozumný
670 shopping centre.......................nákupní středisko
670 balance ....vyvážit/vyrovnat/zůstatek
670 add up ....sečíst
670 bind - bound - bound ...... vázat/zavázat: přítomný
čas - minulý čas - příčestí minulé

LESSON 123

673 notepoznamenat si/poznámka/povšimnout si/tón/
nota/oznámení
673 note down.........................poznamenat si
673 take notes.............................dělat si poznámky
673 notebook..sešit
673 banknote.......................................bankovka
673 key.. klávesa/klíč
673 keyboard.................klávesnice/klávesový nástroj
674 armour ....brnění
674 spread .... šířit
674 all over ....všude
674 fascinated...fascinován
674 scene...místo děje/scéna
674 murderer..vrah
674 evidence .... důkaz
675 i.e. = id est = that is ....i.e. = id est = to je
675 at first.. nejdříve
675 accustomed .... zvyklý

LESSON 124

678 benefit..užitek
678 sake...kvůli/důvod
678 give up ....vzdát se
678 mixed up.............................popletený/smíchaný
678 humour ....humor/nálada
679 dress.. oděv
679 master ....mistr/zvládnout/osvojit si
679 masterpiece.............................mistrovské dílo
679 so... tak, tudíž
679 so that...aby
679 so as to...aby
679 and so on..................................... a tak dál
679 so many...tolik
679 so far .... dosud
679 so far as I know .... pokud vím
681 praise.............................. chválit/pochvala
681 loan...půjčka
681 furthermore.........................kromě toho
681 moreover .... navíc
682 toe .... prst na noze
682 personally .... osobně
682 conscious .... vědomý
682 unconscious ....v bezvědomí
682 self-conscious.................................rozpačitý
682 patient.. pacient

French Vocabulary

LESSON 112

603 joke.........................plaisanter / blaguer / blague
603 pretend ....simuler / faire semblant
603 envelope... enveloppe
603 stamp...timbre
603 leave out...omettre
603 postcode...code postal
604 naturally.. naturellement
604 recent ....récent
604 so-so....................... moyen / comme ci comme ça
604 mate ....copain / copine / pote
604 housemate.......................................colocataire
604 flatmate...colocataire
604 classmate ....camarade de classe
604 workmate...collègue
605 to look forward to...attendre avec impatience / avoir
hâte de
605 let me see.........................laisse(z)-moi réfléchir
606 chance...chance
606 dismiss ....licencier
606 jungle..jungle
606 fifty-fifty.....................cinquante-cinquante
606 take a chance.......................... tenter sa chance
606 whistle ....siffler
606 hunt ....chasser
607 deed ....acte / action
607 grease ....graisse
607 scissors ....ciseaux
607 take control.............................prendre le contrôle
607 lose control.............................perdre le contrôle
607 due .... arriver à échéance / devoir / devoir arriver
607 due to ....dû à / en raison de
608 grandmother....................................... grand-mère
608 grandfather.. grand-père
608 great-grandmother..................arrière-grand-mère
608 great-grandfather....................arrière-grand-père
608 mostly.............principalement / essentiellement /
....pour la plupart
608 totally...totalement
609 sentence..phrase

LESSON 113

610 discuss .... discuter
610 discussion..discussion
610 argue ....se disputer / soutenir /
...................................affirmer / arguer / conclure
610 argument ....dispute / argument
610 quarrel .... se quereller / querelle
610 anger .... colère
611 reason ....raisonner
611 regular ....régulier / ordinaire
611 do something about........................faire quelque
....chose à propos de
611 blow up...........................exploser / faire exploser
612 dust...poussière
612 powder...poudre
612 collect ....s'accumuler / collectionner /
.....................se rassembler / faire une collecte /
....faire la quête
612 face powder.......................poudre pour le visage
612 meeting.............................réunion / meeting
612 football match............................match de football

612 Red Cross ....Croix Rouge
613 furniture ....mobilier / meubles
613 furnish...meubler
613 available ....disponible
613 human being...............................être humain
613 artificial ....artificiel
614 kiss ....bise / baiser (nom) / embrasser
614 rush ....ruée / hâte / affluence
614 hero ....héros

LESSON 114

616 dish...plat
616 serve... servir
616 to be for (or against) something ...... être pour (ou
....contre) quelque chose
616 arms ....armes
616 fox..renard
616 fox hunting............................. chasse au renard
617 seize..s'emparer de / saisir
617 handbag ....sac à main
617 break out ....éclater
617 wage..salaire / paye
617 salary ....salaire
617 payment...paiement
617 profession.. profession
617 non-professional...... non-professionnel / amateur
617 steady.................régulier / stable / ferme / solide
617 seasonal...saisonnier
617 seaside...bord de mer
617 painter ....peintre
617 pianist ....pianiste
617 surgeon .... chirurgien
618 leaf..feuille
618 loaf..pain / miche de pain
618 shelf..étagère
618 cliff...falaise
618 deer ....cerf / daim / biche
618 wood ....bois
619 mention..mentionner
619 tell off...............................gronder / réprimander
619 partner....................................partenaire / associé
619 insist ....insister
620 board ....planche
620 floorboard .... latte de plancher
620 noticeboard........................tableau d'affichage
620 blackboard.......................................tableau noir
620 deck...pont
620 port..port
620 director ....directeur (-trice)

LESSON 115

622 timetable..horaire
622 schedule.........................calendrier / programme
622 account......compte-rendu / compte / comptabilité
623 greedy .... avide
623 satisfied ....satisfait
623 crop ....récolte
623 differ ....différer
623 private..privé
624 what ....ce que
624 whom....................................que / qui (COD)
626 whose..dont

626 search.................................chercher / rechercher
626 support ....soutenir / supporter
627 religious ....religieux

LESSON 116

628 declare...............................déclarer / proclamer
628 red-handed .... en flagrant délit
628 innocent...innocent
628 upper ....supérieur / haut
628 middle...moyen
628 working..ouvrier
628 class...classe
628 society ....société
628 aristocracy ....aristocratie
628 industrialist ....industriel
628 case..............................upper case: majuscule /
....lower case: minuscule
628 lower...inférieur / bas
629 raise...............................soulever / lever / élever
629 to be excused ....être excusé
629 monument ....monument
629 honour ....honneur
629 statue...statue
630 transitive .... transitif
631 respect...respect
631 scorn........ mépris / dédain / mépriser / dédaigner
631 worthy...digne
631 term...trimestre
631 worship...culte
632 cattle ....bétail
632 cowboy ....cowboy / vacher
632 harvest...................................récolte / cueillette
632 mother-in-law..belle-mère
632 father-in-law..beau-père
632 rail..rail
632 railing...............................barrière / balustrade
632 run ....rouler / avancer / fonctionner
632 protection..protection
632 balcony...balcon

LESSON 117

634 knowledge ....savoir / connaissances
634 progress ....progrès
634 item...................................point / article / élément
634 encyclopedia ....encyclopédie
635 mass............masse / the masses: masses, foule
635 advantage..avantage
635 disadvantage....................................inconvénient
635 mass – production ....production de masse
635 production...production
635 product ....produit
635 identical ....identique
635 quality ....qualité
635 pick up ....prendre / venir chercher /
....relever / apprendre
635 date ....rendez-vous (galant)
635 vocabulary...vocabulaire
636 prevent .... éviter / empêcher
636 drum ....tambouriner / bidon / tambour
636 harbour ....port / havre
636 port ....port
637 nosey .... curieux
637 masculine ....masculin
637 feminine.. féminin
637 god ....dieu
637 goddess.. déesse
637 prince.. prince
637 princess..princesse
638 nephew .... neveu

638 niece... nièce
638 landlord..propriétaire
638 landlady ....propriétaire
638 widower .... veuf
638 widow .... veuve
638 event.........................événement / manifestation
638 eventful........mouvementé / riche en évènements
638 uneventful..............tranquille / peu mouvementé /
....sans incidents
638 concern...concerner
639 celebrate....................................fêter / célébrer
639 celebration............................fête / célébrations
639 New Year's Eve...............réveillon du Nouvel An
639 up to date .... à la mode / à jour
639 out of date .... périmé / obsolète
639 essential ....essentiel

LESSON 118

640 article.. article
641 countable ....dénombrable
641 uncountable................................ indénombrable
642 worm...ver
642 silkworm .... ver à soie
642 silk.. soie
642 limb..membre
642 poison.. poison
643 cave....................................caverne / grotte
643 bat.......................................chauve-souris
643 deserve..mériter
643 frequent (verb)....................fréquenter (verbe)
643 frequent (adjective)................fréquent (adjectif)
643 frequently (adverb) .... fréquemment (adverbe)
644 attract...attirer
644 attention.. attention
644 attraction..attrait
644 attractive..attirant
644 good-looking...beau
644 the rest ....le reste
644 miserable.....................malheureux / misérable /
.... piteux / affreux
645 emotion... émotion
645 emotional....................................... émotionnel

LESSON 119

646 firstly...premièrement
646 secondly .... deuxièmement
646 head teacher directeur (-trice) d'école / proviseur
646 study...bureau
647 vote...voter
647 nurse .... soigner
647 nursery ....crèche / garderie / école maternelle
647 unemployment.......................................chômage
647 take off..décoller
647 land..atterrir
647 seat belt..ceinture
648 practice..pratique
648 theory ....théorie
648 practical..pratique
648 take into account ....tenir compte (de) /
....prendre en considération
648 set up...............................fonder / créer / monter
649 nature...nature
649 human nature ....nature humaine
650 compete......................................concurrencer /
.... entrer en concurrence / rivaliser
650 competition......................compétition / concours
650 energy ....énergie
650 efficient...................................efficace / productif
650 suit...aller / convenir

German Vocabulary

LESSON 112

603	joke	Spaß machen / Witz
603	pretend	vorgeben
603	envelope	Briefumschlag
603	stamp	abstempeln / Stempel / Briefmarke
603	leave out	auslassen
603	postcode	Postleitzahl
604	naturally	natürlich
604	recent	letzter / letzte/kürzlich
604	so-so	geht so
604	mate	Kumpel
604	housemate	Mitbewohner/in
604	flatmate	Mitbewohner/in
604	classmate	Klassenkamerad/in
604	workmate	Arbeitskollege/in
605	to look forward to	sich freuen auf
605	let me see	lassen Sie / lass mich mal überlegen
606	chance	Chance
606	dismiss	entlassen
606	jungle	Dschungel
606	fifty-fifty	fifty-fifty
606	take a chance	ein Risiko eingehen
606	whistle	pfeifen
606	hunt	jagen
607	deed	Tat
607	grease	Fett
607	scissors	Schere
607	take control	Kontrolle übernehmen
607	lose control	Kontrolle verlieren
607	due	fällig / dran sein / zu erwarten sein
607	due to	auf Grund von
608	grandmother	Großmutter
608	grandfather	Großvater
608	great-grandmother	Urgroßmutter
608	great-grandfather	Urgroßvater
608	mostly	hauptsächlich
608	totally	völlig
609	sentence	verurteilen

LESSON 113

610	discuss	diskutieren
610	discussion	Diskussion
610	argue	streiten / argumentieren
610	argument	Streit / Argument
610	quarrel	streiten / Streit
610	anger	Ärger
610	reason	argumentieren
611	regular	geregelt
611	do something about	etw. machen gegen
611	blow up	sprengen
612	dust	Staub
612	powder	Pulver
612	collect	ablagern / sammeln / versammeln
612	face powder	Gesichtspuder
612	meeting	Versammlung / Treffen
612	football match	Fußballspiel
612	Red Cross	das Rote Kreuz
613	furniture	Möbel
613	furnish	einrichten
613	available	erhältlich / verfügbar
613	human being	Mensch
613	artificial	künstlich
614	kiss	Kuss / küssen
614	rush	Rush- / sich beeilen
614	hero	Held

LESSON 114

616	dish	Schale / Gericht
616	serve	servieren
616	to be for (or against) something	für (oder gegen) etwas sein
616	arms	Waffen
616	fox	Fuchs
616	fox hunting	Fuchsjagd
617	seize	ergreifen
617	handbag	Handtasche
617	break out	ausbrechen
617	wage	Lohn
617	salary	Gehalt
617	payment	Bezahlung / Zahlung
617	profession	Beruf
617	non-professional	ohne Qualifikation
617	steady	regelmäßig / ruhig / beständig
617	seasonal	Saison- / saisonbedingt
617	seaside	Küsten-
617	painter	Maler
617	pianist	Pianist
617	surgeon	Chirurg
618	leaf	Blatt
618	loaf	Laib
618	shelf	Regal
618	cliff	Klippe
618	deer	Wild
618	wood	Wald
619	mention	erwähnen
619	tell off	ausschimpfen
619	partner	Partner/in
619	insist	auf etw. bestehen
620	board	Brett /an Bord / an Bord gehen / Ausschuss / Gremium / Pension
620	floorboard	Diele
620	noticeboard	Anschlagtafel
620	blackboard	Tafel
620	deck	Deck
620	port	Hafen
620	director	Direktor

LESSON 115

622	timetable	Zeitplan / Fahrplan / Stundenplan
622	schedule	Terminplan / Programm
622	account	Bericht / Konto / Kundenkonto / Protokoll
623	greedy	gierig
623	satisfied	zufrieden
623	crop	Pflanze
623	differ	unterscheiden / abweichen
623	private	privat / Privat-
624	what	was
624	whom	den / die / das
626	whose	dessen / deren
626	search	suchen / durchsuchen
626	support	tragen / unterstützen
627	religious	religiös

LESSON 116

628	declare	erklären / mitteilen
628	red-handed	auf frischer Tat
628	innocent	unschuldig
628	upper	Ober- / Groß / oberer / obere / oberes
628	middle	Mittel-
628	working	Arbeiter-
628	class	Klasse
628	society	Gesellschaft
628	aristocracy	Aristokratie
628	industrialist	Industrieller / Industrielle
628	case	Buchstabe
628	lower	Klein-
629	raise	erheben / aufziehen / züchten / errichten
629	to be excused	entschuldigt sein
629	monument	Denkmal
629	honour	Ehre
629	statue	Statue
630	transitive	transitiv
631	respect	Respekt / einhalten / respektieren
631	scorn	Verachtung
631	worthy	würdig
631	term	Halbjahr / Semester
631	worship	Gottesdienst
632	cattle	Vieh
632	cowboy	Cowboy
632	harvest	Ernte
632	mother-in-law	Schwiegermutter
632	father-in-law	Schwiegervater
632	rail	Schiene
632	railing	Geländer
632	run	fahren / laufen
632	protection	Schutz
632	balcony	Balkon

LESSON 117

634	knowledge	Wissen
634	progress	Fortschritt
634	item	Stück
634	encyclopedia	Lexikon
635	mass	Masse / Massen-
635	advantage	Vorteil
635	disadvantage	Nachteil
635	mass – production	Massenproduktion
635	production	Produktion
635	product	Produkt
635	identical	identisch
635	quality	Qualität
635	pick up	aufheben / abholen / lernen
635	date	Verabredung / Datum
635	vocabulary	Vokabeln
636	prevent	verhindern
636	drum	trommeln/Trommel/Schlagzeug/Fass
636	harbour	Hafen
636	port	Hafen / Hafenstadt
637	nosey	neugierig
637	masculine	maskulin
637	feminine	feminin
637	god	Gott
637	goddess	Göttin
637	prince	Prinz
637	princess	Prinzessin
638	nephew	Neffe
638	niece	Nichte
638	landlord	Vermieter
638	landlady	Vermieterin
638	widower	Witwer
638	widow	Witwe

638	event	Ereignis
638	eventful	ereignisreich
638	uneventful	ereignislos
638	concern	angehen
639	celebrate	feiern
639	celebration	Feier
639	New Year's Eve	Silvester
639	up to date	modern / aktuell
639	out of date	abgelaufen / überholt
639	essential	unerlässlich

LESSON 118

640	article	Artikel
641	countable	zählbar
641	uncountable	unzählbar
642	worm	Wurm
642	silkworm	Seidenraupe
642	silk	Seide
642	limb	Gliedmaße
642	poison	Gift
643	cave	Höhle
643	bat	Fledermaus
643	deserve	verdienen
643	frequent (verb)	besuchen
643	frequent (adjective)	häufig
643	frequently (adverb)	häufig
644	attract	anziehen
644	attention	Aufmerksamkeit
644	attraction	Attraktion
644	attractive	attraktiv
644	good-looking	gutaussehend
644	the rest	der Rest
644	miserable	schlecht / elend
645	emotion	Gefühl
645	emotional	emotional

LESSON 119

646	firstly	erstens
646	secondly	zweitens
646	head teacher	Schulleiter
646	study	Büro
647	vote	wählen
647	nurse	pflegen
647	nursery	Kinderkrippe / Kinderzimmer
647	unemployment	Arbeitslosigkeit
647	take off	abheben
647	land	landen
647	seat belt	Gurt
648	practice	Praxis
648	theory	Theorie
648	practical	praktisch
648	take into account	berücksichtigen
648	set up	gründen
649	nature	Natur
649	human nature	Natur des Menschen
650	compete	konkurrieren
650	competition	Wettbewerb
650	energy	Energie
650	efficient	effizient
650	suit	stehen / passen
650	suitable	geeignet
651	effect	Auswirkung / Wirkung
651	perfect	wildfremd
651	to go up to	zugehen auf
651	sunshine	Sonnenschein

LESSON 120

653	polish	polieren
653	ability	Fähigkeit

682	injection	Spritze
682	gathering	Versammlung
683	split	spalten / reißen / teilen
683	axe	Axt
683	equally	gleich

LESSON 125

684	Alps	die Alpen
684	Andes	die Anden
684	Himalayas	der Himalaya
684	Netherlands	die Niederlande
685	present (noun +adj)	gegenwärtig / anwesend / Geschenk
685	present (verb)	präsentieren
686	swear - swore - sworn	fluchen
687	lazy	faul
687	idle	träge
687	play	Theaterstück
687	scene	Szene
688	verse	Reim / Strophe
688	chorus	Refrain
688	pray	beten
688	prayer	Gebet
688	combine	verbinden
689	heads	Kopf
689	tails	Zahl

LESSON 126

690	extend	gehen / ausstrecken
690	as far as	bis
691	trust	vertrauen / Treuhandkonto
691	dependent	abhängig
691	independent	unabhängig
692	punctual	pünktlich
692	row	rudern
692	oar	Ruder
692	wish	wünschen
693	ideal	ideal
693	theoretical	theoretisch
693	actual	wirklich / tatsächlich
693	actually	in Wirklichkeit
694	check	nachprüfen
694	change	Wechselgeld
694	log	Holzblock
694	fireplace	Kamin
694	common sense	gesunder Menschenverstand
695	tool	Werkzeug
695	bean	Bohne

Italian Vocabulary

LESSON 112

603 joke...scherzare, scherzo
603 pretend ....fingere
603 envelope...busta
603 stamp......................francobollo, timbro, timbrare
603 leave out.............................omettere, tralasciare
603 postcode......................................codice postale
604 naturally.......................................naturalmente
604 recent ....recente
604 so-so...così così
604 mate ....compagno
604 housemate............... compagno d'appartamento,
....coinquilino
604 flatmate.....................compagno d'appartamento
604 classmate ....compagno di classe
604 workmate...............compagno di lavoro, collega
605 to look forward to................... non vedere l'ora di
605 let me see....................................fammi vedere
606 chance............................. opportunità, chance
606 dismiss ....licenziare
606 jungle ....giungla
606 fifty-fifty .... in parti uguali, fare a metà
606 take a chance...rischiare
606 whistle ....fischiare
606 hunt ....caccia
607 deed .... azione
607 grease .... grasso per lubrificare
607 scissors ....forbici
607 take control ....prendere il controllo
607 lose control............................perdere il controllo
607 due ....dovuto, esigibile
607 due to ....dovere, a causa di
608 grandmother.......................................nonna
608 grandfather..nonno
608 great-grandmother..............................bisnonna
608 great-grandfather............................. bisnonno
608 mostly .... per lo più
608 totally..totalmente
609 sentence..... emettere una sentenza, condannare

LESSON 113

610 discuss ....discutere
610 discussion...discussione
610 argue .... litigare, discutere, argomentare
610 argument ....argomento, litigio
610 quarrel ....bisticciare, litigio
610 anger ....collera, ira
610 reason ....argomentare
611 regular ....regolare
611 do something about.................fare qualcosa per
611 blow up ....(far) saltare in aria
612 dust...polvere
612 powder..polvere, cipria
612 collect ....raccogliere, collezionare
612 face powder...cipria
612 meeting...riunione
612 football match............................partita di pallone
612 Red Cross ....Croce Rossa
613 furniture ....mobilio, mobili
613 furnish...arredare
613 available ....disponibile
613 human being..................................essere umano

613 artificial ....artificiale
614 kiss ....bacio, baciare
614 rush ....affrettarsi
614 hero ....eroe

LESSON 114

616 dish..pietanza, piatto
616 serve...servire
616 to be for (or against) something .... essere a
..............................favore di (o contro) qualcosa
616 arms ....armi
616 fox...volpe
616 fox hunting.................................caccia alla volpe
617 seize... afferrare
617 handbag ....borsa
617 break out ....scoppiare
617 wage..paga, salario
617 salary..stipendio
617 payment..pagamento
617 profession...professione
617 non-professional......................non professionale
617 steady.. fisso, fermo
617 seasonal...stagionale
617 seaside ....riva del mare
617 painter ....pittore
617 pianist..pianista
617 surgeon ....chirurgo
618 leaf.. foglia
618 loaf...pagnotta
618 shelf..mensola
618 cliff .... rupe, scogliera
618 deer ....cervo
618 wood...legno
619 mention.. menzionare
619 tell off ....sgridare
619 partner ....socio
619 insist ....insistere
620 board ....tavola, tabella
620 floorboard ....tavola do pavimento
620 noticeboard..bacheca
620 blackboard...lavagna
620 deck...........................ponte delle navi
620 port ....porto
620 director ....direttore

LESSON 115

622 timetable..orario
622 schedule..programma
622 account.................................. resoconto, conto
623 greedy ....avido
623 satisfied ....soddisfatto
623 crop ....coltura, raccolto
623 differ ....differire
623 private..privato
624 what....................................che cosa, cosa, che
624 whom......................................a/con/da cui ecc.
626 whose ....di cui, ecc.
626 search..cercare, ricercare
626 support .... sostenere
627 religious..religioso

Italian vocabulary

LESSON 116

628	declare	dichiarare
628	red-handed	in flagrante
628	innocent	innocente
628	upper	alta
628	middle	media
628	working	operaia (classe)
628	class	classe
628	society	società
628	aristocracy	aristocrazia
628	industrialist	industriale
628	case	lettere (maiuscole, minuscole)
628	lower	minuscole
629	raise	erigere, sollevare
629	to be excused	essere scusato
629	monument	monumento
629	honour	onore
629	statue	statua
630	transitive	transitivo
631	respect	rispetto
631	scorn	disprezzo
631	worthy	degno, meritevole
631	term	trimestre
631	worship	adorare
632	cattle	bestiame
632	cowboy	mandriano
632	harvest	raccolto
632	mother-in-law	suocera
632	father-in-law	suocero
632	rail	rotaia, sbarra
632	railing	ringhiera
632	run	correre
632	protection	protezione
632	balcony	balcone

LESSON 117

634	knowledge	conoscenza
634	progress	progresso
634	item	articolo
634	encyclopedia	enciclopedia
635	mass	massa
635	advantage	vantaggio
635	disadvantage	svantaggio
635	mass-production	massa-produzione
635	production	produzione
635	product	prodotto
635	identical	identico
635	quality	qualità
636	pick up	prendere, andare a prendere, raccogliere, afferrare
636	date	appuntamento
636	vocabulary	vocabolario
636	prevent	prevenire
636	drum	tamburellare, tamburo, bidone
636	harbour	porto, riparo
636	port	porto
637	nosey	curioso, ficcanaso
637	masculine	maschile
637	feminine	femminile
637	god	dio
637	goddess	dea
637	prince	principe
637	princess	prinicipessa
638	nephew	nipote maschio
638	niece	nipote femmina
638	landlord	padrone di casa, proprietario
638	landlady	padrona di casa, proprietaria
638	widower	vedovo
638	widow	vedova
638	event	avvenimento
638	eventful	avventuroso, denso di avvenimenti
638	uneventful	tranquillo, senza incidenti
638	concern	riguardare
639	celebrate	celebrare, festeggiare
639	celebration	celebrazione, festa
639	New Year's eve	vigilia di capodanno
639	up to date	alla moda, aggiornato
639	out of date	fuori moda, scaduto
639	essential	essenziale

LESSON 118

640	article	articolo
641	countable	numerabile
641	uncountable	non numerabile
642	worm	verme, baco, bruco
642	silkworm	baco da seta
642	silk	seta
642	limb	arto
642	poison	veleno
643	cave	caverna
643	bat	pipistrello
643	deserve	meritare
643	frequent (verb)	frequentare
643	frequent (adjective)	frequente
643	frequently (adverb)	frequentemente
643	attract	attrarre
644	attention	attenzione
644	attraction	attrazione
644	attractive	attraente
644	good-looking	di bell'aspetto
644	the rest	il resto
644	miserable	infelice, miserabile, disgraziato
645	emotion	emozione
645	emotional	emotivo

LESSON 119

646	firstly	per prima cosa
646	secondly	successivamente
646	head teacher	preside
646	study	studio
646	vote	votare
647	nurse	curare, badare a
647	nursery	stanza per bambini, giardino di infanzia
647	unemployment	disoccupazione
647	take off	decollare
647	land	atterrare
647	seat belt	cintura di sicurezza
648	practice	pratica
648	theory	teoria
648	practical	pratico
648	take into account	prendere in considerazione
648	set up	metter su, iniziare
649	nature	natura
649	human nature	natura umana
650	compete	competere
650	competition	competizione
650	energy	energia
650	efficient	efficiente
650	suit	adattarsi, andar bene
650	suitable	adatto, conveniente
651	effect	effetto, risultato
651	perfect	perfetto
651	to go up to	avvicinare
651	sunshine	luce del sole

LESSON 120

653 polish .... lucidare
653 ability .... abilità, capacità
653 expense .... costoso
653 postpone .... rinviare
654 stress .... stress
654 stressful .... stressante
654 afterwards .... dopo, più tardi
654 first of all .... prima di tutto
654 attend .... partecipare, presenziare
654 shopkeeper .... negoziante
655 move .... commuovere
655 tear .... lacrima
655 pass .... passare
656 spoil – spoilt – spoilt .... rovinare
656 discipline .... disciplina
656 hunger .... fame
656 share .... dividere

LESSON 121

659 association .... associazione
659 automobile .... automobile
659 disturb .... disturbare
659 concentrate .... concentrare
659 courage .... coraggio
659 virtue .... virtù
660 loyal .... leale
660 loyalty .... lealtà
660 companion .... compagno
660 spirit .... spirito, condiizione di spirito
660 spiritual .... spirituale
660 evil .... perfido, maligno
661 flow .... scorrere
661 festival .... festival
661 feast .... festa, banchetto
661 dare .... osare, sfidare
661 challenge .... sfidare, provocare
662 bring up .... allevare
662 solve .... risolvere
662 calculator .... calcolatrice, calcolatore
663 fix .... fissare, sistemare
663 hammer .... martello
663 nail .... vite
663 fingernail .... unghia
663 criticize .... criticare

LESSON 122

665 yard .... corte, cortile
665 courtyard .... cortile
665 enclose .... recintare
665 space .... spazio
665 amuse .... divertire, distrarsi
665 comical .... comico
665 pass (the time) .... passare
665 cards .... carte
665 waiting room .... sala d'attesa
665 amusement .... divertimento
666 hobby .... hobby
666 photography .... fotografia
666 order .... ordine
666 pack .... fare i bagagli, stipare
666 packed .... affollato
666 suitcase .... valigia
666 shorts .... calzoncini corti
666 T-shirt .... maglietta
667 thorn .... spina
667 rose .... rosa
667 afford .... permettersi

667 agreement .... patto, accordo
667 basket .... cesto
667 trolley .... carrello
667 nut .... noci (di tutti i tipi)
668 regarding .... che riguarda
668 material .... materiale
668 duvet .... piumino
668 cotton .... cotone
668 leather .... pelle
668 convenience .... comodità
668 convenient .... comodo
668 inconvenient .... scomodo
668 inconvenience .... disturbo
668 dining room .... sala da pranzo
668 sensitive .... sensibile, sensitivo
668 offend .... offendere
668 criticism .... critica
668 thermometer .... termometro
669 sensible .... sensato, di buon senso
669 reasonable .... ragionevole
670 shopping centre .... centro commerciale
670 balance .... tenere in equilibrio, pareggiare
670 add up .... addizionare
670 bind – bound – bound .... legare, vincolare ecc.

LESSON 123

673 note .... annotare, osservare, nota
673 note down .... annotare, trascrivere
673 take notes .... prendere appunti
673 notebook .... taccuino
673 banknote .... banconota
673 key .... tasto
673 keyboard .... tastiera
674 armour .... armatura, corazza
674 spread .... stendere, diffondere
674 all over .... dappertutto
674 fascinated .... affascinato
674 scene .... scena
674 murderer .... assassino
674 evidence .... prove
675 i.e. = id est = that is .. i.e. (id est): cioè, vale a dire
675 at first .... in principio, dapprima
675 accustomed .... abituato

LESSON 124

678 benefit .... vantaggio, beneficio
678 sake .... per, motivo, amore
678 give up .... rinunciare
678 mixed up .... confuso
678 humour .... umore
679 dress .... abbigliamento
679 master .... maestro, conoscere a fondo
679 masterpiece .... capolavoro
679 so .... così
679 so that .... cosicché
679 so as to .... in modo da
679 and so on .... e così via
679 so many .... cosí tanti
679 so far .... fino ad ora
679 so far as I know .... per quanto ne so
681 praise .... lodare, elogiare
681 loan .... prestito
681 furthermore .... inoltre
681 moreover .... per di più, in aggiunta
682 toe .... dito del piede
682 personally .... personalmente
682 conscious .... consapevole, cosciente
682 unconscious .... inconsapevole, inconscio
682 self-conscious .... impacciato

682 patient...paziente
682 injection ....iniezione
682 gathering ....raduno
683 split...dividere
683 axe...ascia
683 equally............................ ugualmente, altrettanto

LESSON 125

684 Alps ....Alpi
684 Andes ....Ande
684 Himalayas...Himalaya
684 Netherlands .... Paesi Bassi
685 present (noun +adj)............. il presente, presente
685 present (verb)......................................presentare
686 swear – swore – sworn........................imprecare
687 lazy..pigro
687 idle...inattivo, in ozio
687 play...commedia
687 scene... scena
688 verse.. verso
688 chorus...coro
688 pray ....pregare
688 prayer ....preghiera
688 combine..combinare
689 heads..testa (di moneta)
689 tails...croce (di moneta)

LESSON 126

690 extend...estendere
690 as far as... fino a
691 trust .... avere fiducia in, fidarsi
691 dependent .... dipendente
691 independent.................................... indipendente
692 punctual...puntuale
692 row...remare, vogare
692 oar ....remo
692 wish .... desiderio
693 ideal.. ideale
693 theoretical...teorico
693 actual...reale, vero
693 actually ....veramente
694 check.....................................accertarsi, verificare
694 change..resto
694 log..ciocco, ceppo
694 fireplace.....................................camino, focolare
694 common sense .... buon senso
695 tool..utensile
695 bean ....fagiolo

Japanese Vocabulary

LESSON 112

603 joke..冗談を言う；冗談
603 pretend ....振りをする；まねをして遊ぶ
603 envelope..封筒
603 stamp.............切手；スタンプ；スタンプで押す
603 leave out.........................省く，そのままにしておく
603 postcode..郵便番号
604 naturally...................自然に；もちろん，当然
604 recent ....最近の
604 so-so................................まあまあ，まずまず
604 mate...仲間
604 housemate..同居人
604 flatmate......................................フラットメート
604 classmate................................クラスメート
604 workmate..仕事仲間
605 to look forward to..................... を楽しみに待つ
605 let me see... ええと
606 chance..機会；見込み
606 dismiss..解雇する
606 jungle...ジャングル
606 fifty-fifty.......................................五分五分の
606 take a chance.....................................運に任せる
606 whistle ....口笛を吹く
606 hunt ....狩猟する
607 deed ....行為
607 grease ....グリース
607 scissors ....はさみ
607 take control ....コントロールする
607 lose control............コントロールできなくなる
607 due支払期日のきた；...することになって：到着予定で
607 due to ....の理由で
608 grandmother...祖母
608 grandfather...祖父
608 great-grandmother...............................曾祖母
608 great-grandfather...............................曾祖父
608 mostly.......................................たいていは
608 totally...完全に
609 sentence................................判決を宣告する

LESSON 113

610 discuss ....論議する
610 discussion..討論
610 argue ....論争する；説得する
610 argument..論争
610 quarrel..口論する
610 anger ....怒り
610 reason ....説得してさせる
611 regular ....規則正しい
611 do something about.....................を何とかする
611 blow up ....爆破させる
612 dust...ほこり
612 powder...粉，粉末
612 collect.. たまる；収集する；集まる；寄付を募る
612 face powder...おしろい
612 meeting..会議
612 football match..........................サッカー試合
612 Red Cross ....赤十字
613 furniture..家具
613 furnish..家具付きの
613 available入手できる；（手が空いていて）対応できる

613 human being......................................人間
613 artificial ....人工的な
614 kiss ....キスする；キス
614 rush .... ラッシュ，異常な数量；急いで行く
614 hero .... ヒーロー，英雄

LESSON 114

616 dish..................................大盛り皿；料理
616 serve..................................食事を配膳する
616 to be for (or against) something ..何かに賛成（反対）する
616 arms ....武器
616 fox...狐
616 fox hunting ....狐狩り
616 seize ....つかみ取る
617 handbag ....ハンドバック
617 break out ....急に発生する
617 wage...賃金
617 salary...給料
617 payment...報酬
617 profession....................（頭脳を用いる）専門職
617 non - professional............................非専門職的な
617 steady ....安定した；着実な
617 seasonal...季節的な
617 seaside...海辺の
617 painter...画家
617 pianist..ピアニスト
617 surgeon ....外科医
618 leaf...（木などの）葉
618 loaf..............................（パンなどの）ひと塊り
618 shelf ....棚
618 cliff ....崖
618 deer ....鹿
618 wood ....森
619 mention ....話に出す
619 tell off ....ひどくしかる
619 partner...パートナー
619 insist ....主張する，言い張る
620 board板；乗り込む；搭乗して；取締役会；食事つき
620 floorboard ....床板
620 noticeboard...掲示板
620 blackboard...黒板
620 deck ....デッキ
620 port ....港
620 director ....取締役

LESSON 115

622 timetable...時間割
622 schedule...スケジュール
622 account....... 説明；口座；掛け売り勘定；会計簿
623 greedy ....欲張りな
623 satisfied ....満足した
623 crop...作物
623 differ ....異なる
623 private...プライベートの
624 what....................................（...する）こと / もの
624 whom .... するところの人
626 whose...その物 / 人の...が
626 search......... 捜索する；（人を）所持品検査する
626 support ....支える；支持する
627 religious..宗教の

Japanese vocabulary

LESSON 116

628	declare	断言する，；布告する，言明する
628	red-handed	現行犯で
628	innocent	無罪の
628	upper	上流の；大文字の；上部の
628	middle	中流の
628	working	労働者の
628	class	階級
628	society	社会
628	aristocracy	貴族
628	industrialist	実業家
628	case	格
628	lower	小文字の；下げる
629	raise	持ち上げる；上げる；育てる；立てる
629	to be excused	退室の許しを得る
629	monument	記念碑
629	honour	敬意
629	statue	像
630	transitive	他動詞の
631	respect	尊敬
631	scorn	軽蔑
631	worthy	値する
631	term	学期
631	worship	崇拝する
632	cattle	家畜
632	cowboy	カーボーイ
632	harvest	収穫
632	mother-in-law	義理の母
632	father-in-law	義理の父
632	rail	レール
632	railing	手すり；さく
632	run	走る
632	protection	保護
632	balcony	バルコニー

LESSON 117

634	knowledge	知識
634	progress	進歩
634	item	品目
634	encyclopedia	百科事典
635	mass	大衆
635	advantage	利点
635	disadvantage	不利な点
635	mass – production	大量生産
635	production	プロダクション，生産
635	product	製品
635	identical	同一の
635	quality	品質
635	pick up	拾い上げる；迎えに行く；聞き覚える
635	date	デート
635	vocabulary	語彙
636	prevent	防ぐ
636	drum	コツコツたたく；ドラム
636	harbour	（船の停泊場所としての）港
636	port	商港；港町
637	nosey	詮索好きな
637	masculine	男性の
637	feminine	女性の
637	god	男神
637	goddess	女神
637	prince	王子
637	princess	王女
638	nephew	甥
638	niece	姪
638	landlord	（男の）家主，主人
638	landlady	（女の）家主，主人
638	widower	おとこやもめ
638	widow	未亡人

638	event	出来事；イベント
638	eventful	波乱に富む
638	uneventful	平穏無事な
638	concern	関係する
639	celebrate	祝う
639	celebration	祝賀
639	New Year's Eve	大晦日
639	up to date	最新の
639	out of date	期限切れの
639	essential	不可欠の

LESSON 118

640	article	冠詞
641	countable	数えられる，可算の
641	uncountable	数えられない，不可算の
642	worm	虫
642	silkworm	蚕
642	silk	絹
642	limb	手足
642	poison	毒薬
643	cave	洞穴
643	bat	コウモリ
643	deserve	を受けるに値する
643	frequent (verb)	しばしば行く
643	frequent (adjective)	たびたびの
643	frequently (adverb)	頻繁に
644	attract	（注意を）引く
644	attention	注意
644	attraction	人を引き付けるもの，アトラクション
644	attractive	魅力的な
644	good-looking	美形な
644	the rest	その他の
644	miserable	みじめな；みずぼらしい；憂鬱な
645	emotion	感情
645	emotional	感情的な

LESSON 119

646	firstly	第一に
646	secondly	第二に
646	head teacher	校長
646	study	（個人）事務室，書斎
647	vote	投票する
647	nurse	注意して扱う；看護する
647	nursery	託児所
647	unemployment	失業（状態）
647	take off	離陸する
647	land	着陸する
647	seat belt	シートベルト
648	practice	実践
648	theory	理論
648	practical	実用的な
648	take into account	を考慮に入れる
648	set up	商売を始める
649	nature	性質
649	human nature	人の本性
650	compete	競争する
650	competition	コンクール，コンテスト
650	energy	活力；エネルギー
650	efficient	効率のよい
650	suit	に合う；好都合である
650	suitable	適した
651	effect	影響
651	perfect	まったくの
651	to go up to	に近づいていく
651	sunshine	日差し

LESSON 120

653	polish	磨く
653	ability	能力
653	expense	経費
653	postpone	延期する
654	stress	ストレス
654	stressful	ストレスの多い
654	afterwards	その後
654	first of all	まず第一に
654	attend	出席する；対応する；注意して聞く
654	shopkeeper	店主
655	move	感動させる
655	tear	涙
655	making requests	
655	pass	手渡す
656	spoil - spoilt - spoilt	台無しにする；甘やかす
656	discipline	しつけ
656	hunger	空腹
656	share	分け合う；株

LESSON 121

659	association	協会
659	automobile	自動車の
659	disturb	邪魔する
659	concentrate	集中する
659	courage	勇気
659	virtue	美徳
660	loyal	忠実な
660	loyalty	忠誠
660	companion	つれ, 仲間
660	spirit	精神；霊魂：霊；気分；蒸留酒
660	spiritual	霊的な
660	evil	邪悪な
661	flow	流れ；流れる
661	festival	祝祭, フェスティバル
661	feast	大ごちそう
661	dare	あえて…する；（…するように）挑戦する
661	challenge	挑む
662	bring up	育てる
662	solve	解く
662	calculator	電卓
663	fix	固定する；決める
663	hammer	かなづち
663	nail	くぎ
663	fingernail	爪
663	criticize	批評する, あらを探す, 非難する

LESSON 122

665	yard	囲い地
665	courtyard	中庭
665	enclose	囲む
665	space	空間
665	amuse	楽しませる；楽しく時間を過ごさせる
665	comic	喜劇の
665	pass (the time)	（時間を）過ごす
665	cards	トランプ
665	waiting room	待合室
665	amusement	遊戯施設
666	hobby	趣味
666	photography	写真撮影
666	order	順番
666	pack	荷物を詰める
666	packed	すし詰めの
666	suitcase	スーツケース
666	shorts	半ズボン
666	T-shirt	ティーシャツ
667	thorn	トゲ
667	rose	バラ

667	afford	する余裕がある
667	agreement	協定
667	basket	かご, バスケット
667	trolley	手押し車
667	nut	木の実, ナッツ
668	regarding	について
668	material	材質
668	duvet	掛け布団
668	cotton	綿
668	leather	革
668	convenience	便利；便利な施設や物；好都合
668	convenient	便利な
668	inconvenient	不便な
668	inconvenience	不便
668	dining room	食堂
668	sensitive	感度のよい；敏感に反応する；傷つきやすい
668	offend	感情を害する
668	criticism	非難, 批判
668	thermometer	温度計
669	sensible	分別のある
669	reasonable	道理にかなった
670	shopping centre	ショッピングセンター
670	balance	バランスを取る；帳尻が合う；残り
670	add up	加算する
670	bind - bound - bound	縛る；包帯をする；製本する；拘束する

LESSON 123

673	note	メモを取る；メモ；気付く；音；短信
673	note down	書き留める
673	take notes	ノートを取る
673	notebook	帳面, ノート
673	banknote	紙幣
673	key	キー
673	keyboard	鍵盤
674	armour	鎧兜, 甲冑
674	spread	広がる
674	all over	全体にわたって
674	fascinated	興味をそそられて
674	scene	現場
674	murderer	殺人犯
674	evidence	証拠
675	i.e. = id est = that is	言い換えれば
675	at first	最初は
675	accustomed	慣れた

LESSON 124

678	benefit	恩恵
678	sake	ため
678	give up	やめる
678	mixed up	混乱する, ごちゃごちゃになる
678	humour	ユーモア
679	dress	服装
679	master	名人, 名匠；習得する
679	masterpiece	傑作
679	so	それで
679	so that	するために
679	so as to	するために
679	and so on	など
679	so many	こんなにたくさんの
679	so far	いままでのところ
679	so far as I know	知っている限り
681	praise	ほめる；ほめること
681	loan	ローン
681	furthermore	その上に
681	moreover	さらに
682	toe	足指
682	personally	個人的に

Polish Vocabulary

LESSON 112

603 joke.................................. żartować, żart, dowcip
603 pretend ....udawać
603 envelope...koperta
603 stamp................znaczek, pieczątka, stemplować
603 leave out.. pominąć
603 postcode...kod pocztowy
604 naturally...naturalnie
604 recent ....ostatni
604 so-so...................................... tak sobie, taki sobie
604 mate ....kumpel
604 housemate.......................................współlokator
604 flatmate...współlokator
604 classmate .... kolega z klasy
604 workmate..............................znajomy z pracy
605 to look forward to...............................oczekiwać
605 let me see...............chwileczkę, niech pomyśle
606 chance...szansa
606 dismiss ....zwolnić
606 jungle..dżungla
606 fifty-fifty..pół na pół
606 take a chance.....................skorzystać z okazji
606 whistle ....gwizdać
606 hunt ....polować
607 deed .... czyn, uczynek
607 grease .... smar, tłuszcz
607 scissors ....nożyczki
607 take control............................przejąć kontrolę
607 lose control.................................stracić kontrole
607 due .... należy, należny
607 due to ....z powodu, spowodowany
608 grandmother... babcia
608 grandfather..dziadek
608 great-grandmother............................. prababcia
608 great-grandfather.............................. pradziadek
608 mostly...........................przeważnie, głównie
608 totally .... całkowicie, kompletnie
609 sentence...skazać kogoś

LESSON 113

610 discuss ....dyskutować
610 discussion..dyskusja
610 argue ....spierać się, argumentować
610 argument ....sprzeczka
610 quarrel ....kłótnia, kłócić się
610 anger ....złość
610 reason ....rozumować
611 regular ....regularny
611 do something about..............zrobić coś, zaradzić
611 blow up .... wysadzić w powietrze
612 dust... kurz
612 powder... proszek
612 collect ....zbierać
612 face powder..puder
612 meeting...spotkanie
612 football match....................mecz piłki nożnej
612 Red Cross .... czerwony krzyż
613 furniture .... meble
613 furnish...umeblować
613 available ....dostępny
613 human being..................................istota ludzka
613 artificial ....sztuczny

614 kiss ....całować, pocałunek
614 rush .... pośpiech, spieszyć sie
614 hero...bohater

LESSON 114

616 dish..............półmisek, naczynie, potrawa, danie
616 serve....................................nakładać, serwować
616 to be for (or against) something ....być za
.... (przeciw) czymś (czemuś)
616 arms ....broń
616 fox...lis
616 fox hunting............................polowanie na lisy
617 seize .... łapać, chwytać
617 handbag..torebka
617 break out ....wybuchnąć
617 wage...zapłata
617 salary ....pensja
617 payment...opłata
617 profession..zawód
617 non - professional....................nieprofesjonalny
617 steady...stabilny, stały
617 seasonal ....sezonowy
617 seaside ....wybrzeże morza
617 painter ....malarz
617 pianist ....pianista
617 surgeon ....chirurg
618 leaf...liść
618 loaf...bochenek
618 shelf... półka
618 cliff...urwisko skalne, klif
618 deer..jeleń
618 wood...las
619 mention..wspomnieć
619 tell off...zganić
619 partner...partner
619 insist .... nalegać
620 board .... deska, wsiadać, rada
620 floorboard .... deska podłogowa, panel
620 noticeboard...........................tablica informacyjna
620 blackboard..tablica
620 deck... pokład
620 port...port
620 director ....dyrektor

LESSON 115

622 timetable.. rozkład
622 schedule..harmonogram
622 account..................................relacja, konto
623 greedy .... chciwy, zachłanny
623 satisfied ....zadowolony, usatysfakcjonowany
623 crop ....plon
623 differ ....różnić się
623 private...prywatny
624 what.. co
624 whom ....który (osoba)
626 whose.......................................którego (osoba)
626 search................................szukać, przeszukać
626 support ....wspierać, podeprzeć
627 religious...religijny

LESSON 116

628 declare......................................deklarować (się),
....wypowiadać, ogłaszać

628 red-handed ....złapany na gorącym uczynku
628 innocent...niewinny
628 upper ....wyższy, górny
628 middle..średni
628 working ....pracujący
628 class ....klasa
628 society ....społeczeństwo
628 aristocracy ....arystokracja
628 industrialist .... przemysłowiec
628 case ....czcionka
628 lower ....niższy, obniżać
629 raise....................wznieść, wychować, hodować
629 to be excused .... być usprawiedliwionym
629 monument .... pomnik
629 honour ....honor
629 statue..posąg
630 transitive .... przechodni
631 respect...................................szacunek, respekt
631 scorn......................... pogarda, lekceważenie
631 worthy................................zasługujący, godny
631 term .... semestr
631 worship.............................. wielbić, czcić
632 cattle.. bydło
632 cowboy..kowboj
632 harvest..żniwa
632 mother-in-law.....................................teściowa
632 father-in-law.. teść
632 rail.. pręt, szyna
632 railing.............................. ogrodzenie, balustrada
632 run ....jechać
632 protection.................... ochrona, bezpieczeństwo
632 balcony ....balkon

LESSON 117
634 knowledge ....wiedza
634 progress ....postęp
634 item..sztuka
634 encyclopedia .... encyklopedia
635 mass..masa, masowy
635 advantage...korzyść
635 disadvantage...................................niekorzyść
635 mass-production.................... produkcja masowa
635 production.. produkcja
635 product ....produkt
635 identical ....identyczny
635 quality..jakość
636 pick up ....podnieść, zabrać, nauczać się
636 date ....randka
636 vocabulary ....słownictwo
636 prevent ....zapobiec
636 drum ....bębnić, beczka, bęben
636 harbour .... przystań
636 port ....port
637 nosey............................wścibski, ciekawski
637 masculine ....męski
637 feminine...żeński
637 god ....bóg
637 goddess.. bogini
637 prince...książę
637 princess...księżniczka
638 nephew................... siostrzeniec, bratanek
638 niece................................ siostrzenica, bratanica
638 landlord............ właściciel domu czynszowego
638 landlady........... właścicielka domu czynszowego
638 widower .... wdowiec
638 widow ....wdowa
638 event....................wydarzenie, dyscyplina sportu
638 eventful..urozmaicony

638 uneventful...monotonny
638 concern...dotyczyć
639 celebrate........................ świętować, celebrować
639 celebration ....obchód
639 New Year's Eve .... Sylwester
639 up to date ....ważne, modne
639 out of date .... nieważne, przestarzałe
639 essential .... niezbędny, istotny

LESSON 118
640 article...rodzajnik
641 countable... policzalny
641 uncountable............................... niepoliczalny
642 worm...robak, glista
642 silkworm..jedwabnik
642 silk...jedwab
642 limb............................. kończyna, członek ciała
642 poison...trucizna
643 cave..jaskinia
643 bat .... nietoperz
643 deserve .... zasługiwać
643 frequent (verb).............................. uczęszczać
643 frequent (adjective)..................................częsty
643 frequently (adverb) ....często
643 attract ....przyciągać
644 attraction.. atrakcja
644 attractive...atrakcyjny
644 attention.. uwaga
644 good-looking...urodziwy
644 the rest ....reszta
644 miserable............nieszczęśliwy, nędzny, żałosny
644 emotion.. emocja
645 emotional..emocjonalny

LESSON 119
646 firstly...po pierwsze
646 secondly ....po drugie
646 head teacher ....dyrektor szkoły
646 study.. gabinet
646 vote..głosować
647 nurse .... pielęgnować, opiekować się
647 nursery ....żłobek
647 unemployment..................................... bezrobocie
647 take off..start (samolotu)
647 land..lądować
647 seat belt.............................pasy bezpieczeństwa
648 practice.. praktyka
648 theory ....teoria
648 practical...praktyczny
648 take into account .... wziąć pod uwagę
648 set up..założyć
649 nature ....natura
649 human nature .... natura ludzka
650 compete............................... współzawodniczyć
650 competition .... zawody, konkurs
650 energy ....energia
650 efficient................................. sprawny, wydajny
650 suit...........................pasować, odpowiadać
650 suitable..odpowiednie
651 effect..skutek, efekt
651 perfect .... zupełny, całkowity
651 to go up to ....podejść
651 sunshine...słońce

LESSON 120
653 polish..polerować
653 ability ....umiejętność
653 expense...wydatek
653 postpone...............odłożyć, przesunąć (w czasie)

Polish vocabulary

682 gathering .... zebranie
683 split .... rozszczepić, rozpruć, rozdzielić
683 axe..siekiera
683 equally .... równo

LESSON 125

684 Alps ....Alpy
684 Andes ....Andy
684 Himalayas...Himalaje
684 Netherlands ....Holandia
685 present (noun +adj) ....obecny, prezent
685 present (verb).............. podarować, prezentować
686 swear – swore – sworn..................................kląć
687 lazy...leniwy
687 idle..............................leniwy, bezczynny, próżny
687 play..sztuka
687 scene...scena
688 verse...werset, zwrotka
688 chorus..refren
688 pray ....modlić się
688 prayer ....modlitwa
688 combine..po/łączyć
689 heads...orzeł
689 tails.. reszka

LESSON 126

690 extend......................... ciągnąć się, wyciągnąć
690 as far as..aż do
691 trust ....ufać, zaufanie
691 dependent ....zależny
691 independent...niezależny
692 punctual..punktualnie
692 row...wiosłować
692 oar ....wiosło
692 wish ....chcieć, pragnąć
693 ideal..idealny
693 theoretical...teoretyczny
693 actual.................................rzeczywisty, faktyczny
693 actually ....rzeczywiście,
          .... w rzeczywistości, faktycznie
693 check ....sprawdzić
693 change.. reszta
694 log...bal, belka
694 fireplace..kominek
694 common sense .... zdrowy rozsądek
695 tool.. narzędzie
695 bean .... fasola

Portuguese Vocabulary

LESSON 112

603 joke.. gracejar / piada
603 pretend ....fingir
603 envelope.. envelope
603 stamp.. selo / carimbar
603 leave out.......................................deixar de fora
603 postcode...................................código postal
604 naturally.................................... naturalmente
604 recent ....recente
604 so-so....................................mais ou menos
604 mate .... amigo
604 housemate......................companheiro de casa
604 flatmate....................companheiro de casa
604 classmate ....companheiro de sala de aula
604 workmate.................. companheiro de trabalho
605 to look forward to...........ansiosos para (positivo)
605 let me see..................me dê tempo para pensar
606 chance............................ oportunidade / chance
606 dismiss .... demitir
606 jungle..selva
606 fifty-fifty.............................. meio a meio
606 take a chance.................tentar a sorte / arriscar
606 whistle ....assoviar
606 hunt .... caçar
607 deed .... ação
607 grease ....graxa
607 scissors ....tesoura
607 take control.........................assumir o controle
607 lose control ....perder o controle
607 due .... previsto
607 due to .... devido a
608 grandmother.................................... avó
608 grandfather...................................... avô
608 great-grandmother......................bisavó
608 great-grandfather......................bisavô
608 mostly.. na maioria
608 totally...totalmente
609 sentence... sentenciar

LESSON 113

610 discuss ....discutir
610 discussion...................................discussão
610 argue .... argumentar / discutir
610 argument ....discussão / argumento
610 quarrel .... brigar / disputar
610 anger .... raiva
610 reason .... raciocinar
611 regular .... regular / usual
611 do something about............ fazer algo à respeito
611 blow up.................................... explodir
612 dust..poeira
612 powder...pó
612 collect .... coletar
612 face powder.................................... pó-de-arroz
612 meeting..reunião
612 football match............................ jogo de futebol
612 Red Cross .... cruz vermelha
613 furniture ....mobília / móveis
613 furnish .... mobiliar
613 available ....disponível
613 human being............................... ser humano
613 artificial ....artificial

LESSON 114

614 kiss ....beijar / beijo
614 rush ....apressar-se
614 hero ....herói

LESSON 114

616 dish...prato
616 serve.. servir
616 to be for (or against) something ....a favor
.... (ou contra) alguma coisa
616 arms ....armas
616 fox...raposa
616 fox hunting .... caça à raposa
617 seize ....pegar à força
617 handbag .... bolsa
617 break out .... eclodir (começar)
617 wage..salário
617 salary..salário
617 payment...pagamento
617 profession.. profissão
617 non-professional...........amador / não profissional
617 steady...estável / fixo
617 seasonal....................temporário, de temporada
617 seaside .... litoral
617 painter .... pintor
617 pianist...pianista
617 surgeon .... cirurgião
618 leaf...folha
618 loaf...pão
618 shelf... prateleira
618 cliff .... penhasco
618 deer.. veado
618 wood...bosque
619 mention... mencionar
619 tell off............................. repreender / dar bronca
619 partner...sócio
619 insist ....insistir
620 board .... quadro / tábua / conselho
620 floorboard ....assoalho
620 noticeboard.............................quadro de avisos
620 blackboard..lousa
620 deck..convés
620 port..porto
620 director ....diretor

LESSON 115

622 timetable...horário
622 schedule............................... horário / programa
622 account.. conta
623 greedy .... ganancioso / guloso
623 satisfied ....satisfeito
623 crop ....colheita
623 differ .... diferir / diferenciar
623 private... privado
624 what..que
624 whom...quem
626 whose..de quem
626 search.................................... procurar / busca
626 support .... sustentar, apoiar
627 religious...religioso

LESSON 116

628 declare................................. declarar, proclamar
628 red-handed.....................................pego no ato

628 innocent...inocente
628 upper.........................alto / mais alto / superior
628 middle...média
628 working................................trabalhadora/ baixa
628 class..classe
628 society..sociedade
628 aristocracy..aristocracia
628 industrialist..industrial
628 case...letra
628 lower..minúscula
629 raise......................................criar / levantar
629 to be excused .... ser desculpado, receber licença
629 monument ....monumento
629 honour ....honra
629 statue... estátua
630 transitive..transitivo
631 respect... respeito
631 scorn..desprezo
631 worthy.....................................digno / merecedor
631 term.......................................termo (semestre)
631 worship.. louvar, venerar
632 cattle..gado
632 cowboy .... vaqueiro
632 harvest...colheita
632 mother-in-law..sogra
632 father-in-law...sogro
632 rail...trilho
632 railing..............................grade, corrimão
632 run...correr
632 protection...proteção
632 balcony .... sacada

LESSON 117

634 knowledge ....conhecimento
634 progress ....progresso
634 item...item
634 encyclopedia ....enciclopédia
635 mass....................................em massa / maioria
635 advantage...vantagem
635 disadvantage.................................. desvantagem
635 mass-production................. produção em massa
635 production..produção
635 product ....produto
635 identical ....idêntico
635 quality .... qualidade
636 pick up..pegar / captar
636 date ....encontro
636 vocabulary.......................................vocabulário
636 prevent ....prevenir
636 drum ....bater (tocar) – tambor / barril
636 harbour..porto
636 port...porto
637 nosey..intrometido
637 masculine ....masculino
637 feminine .... feminino
637 god ....Deus
637 goddess.. deusa
637 prince...princípe
637 princess .... princesa
638 nephew...sobrinho
638 niece.. sobrinha
638 landlord..proprietário
638 landlady..proprietária
638 widower ....viúvo
638 widow..viúva
638 event... evento
638 eventful...agitado
638 uneventful.................................. rotineiro / calmo

638 concern..preocupar
639 celebrate...celebrar
639 celebration... celebração
639 New Year's Eve .... véspera de ano novo
639 up to date .... na moda (recente) / válido
639 out of date ....fora de moda, inválido
639 essential ....essencial

LESSON 118

640 article...artigo
641 countable..contável
641 uncountable...incontável
642 worm...verme
642 silkworm .... bicho-da-seda
642 silk ....seda
642 limb...membro
642 poison .... veneno
643 cave... caverna
643 bat ....morcego
643 deserve..merecer
643 frequent (verb)...............................freqüentar
643 frequent (adjective).............................freqüente
643 frequently (adverb) ....freqüentemente
643 attract ....atrair
644 attention...atenção
644 attraction...atração
644 attractive..atraente
644 good-looking.. bonito
644 the rest .... os outros
644 miserable..miserável
644 emotion..emoção
645 emotional...........................emotivo / emocional

LESSON 119

646 firstly...primeiramente
646 secondly .... em secundo lugar
646 head teacher ....professor principal
646 study..estudar
646 vote..votar
647 nurse .... acalentar, cuidar de, enfermeira
647 nursery..berçário
647 unemployment.................................desemprego
647 take off...decolar
647 land...aterrissar
647 seat belt...........................cinto de segurança
648 practice .... prática
648 theory ....teoria
648 practical .... prático
648 take into account ....levar em consideração
648 set up..começar
649 nature ....natureza
649 human nature ....natureza humana
650 compete...competir
650 competition ....competição
650 energy...energia
650 efficient..eficiente
650 suit............................ combinar / servir / adequar
650 suitable..adequado
651 effect.. efeito
651 perfect ....perfeito (completo)
651 to go up to .... ir em direção à
651 sunshine ....brilho do sol

LESSON 120

653 polish .... polir
653 ability .... capacidade / habilidade
653 expense .... gasto
653 postpone...adiar
654 stress... estresse

LESSON 121

LESSON 122

LESSON 123

LESSON 124

683 axe.. machado
683 equally .... igualmente

LESSON 125

684 Alps ....Alpes
684 Andes ....Andes
684 Himalayas... Himalaias
684 Netherlands ....Países Baixos, Holanda
685 present (noun +adj)............ presente (subs + adj)
685 present (verb)........................ presentear (verbo)
686 swear – swore – sworn.........................praguejar
.... – praguejou – praguejado
687 lazy .... preguiçoso
687 idle.. inativo / inútil
687 play.. peça teatral
687 scene... cena
688 verse.. verso
688 chorus...coro / refrão
688 pray .... rezar (orar)
688 prayer ....prece (oração)
688 combine .... combinar
689 heads..cara
689 tails...coroa

LESSON 126

690 extend..estender (ir até)
690 as far as..ir até
691 trust .... confiar
691 dependent .... dependente
691 independent.................................... idependente
692 punctual.. pontual
692 row..remar
692 oar ....remo
692 wish .... desejar
693 ideal.. ideal
693 theoretical.. teórico
693 actual..real
693 actually ....realmente
693 check..checar (conferir)
693 change...troco
694 log..lenha
694 fireplace..lareira
694 common sense .... bom senso
695 tool...ferramenta
695 bean .... feijãot

Russian Vocabulary

LESSON 112

603	joke	шутка, шутить
603	pretend	притворяться
603	envelope	конверт
603	stamp	печать, почтовая марка
603	leave out	пропускать
603	postcode	почтовый индекс
604	naturally	непринужденно, естественно
604	recent	последний, недавний
604	so-so	так себе
604	mate	друг
604	housemate	сосед по дому
604	flatmate	сосед по квартире
604	classmate	одноклассник
604	workmate	сотрудник
605	to look forward to	с нетерпением ожидать
605	let me see	дайте подумать
606	chance	шанс
606	dismiss	увольнять
606	jungle	джунгли
606	fifty-fifty	пятьдесят на пятьдесят
606	take a chance	рискнуть
606	whistle	свистеть
606	hunt	охотиться
607	deed	поступок
607	grease	смазка
607	scissors	ножницы
607	take control	брать управление
607	lose control	терять управление
607	due	надлежащий, должный
607	due to	из-за
608	grandmother	бабушка
608	grandfather	дедушка
608	great-grandmother	прабабушка
608	great-grandfather	прадедушка
608	mostly	в основном
608	totally	абсолютно
609	sentence	приговаривать

LESSON 113

610	discuss	обсуждать
610	discussion	обсуждение
610	argue	спорить
610	argument	спор
610	quarrel	ссориться, ссора
610	anger	гнев
610	reason	излагать мотивы, рассуждать, аргументировать
611	regular	регулярный, систематический, постоянный
611	do something about	предпринимать что-то относительно
611	blow up	взрывать
612	dust	пыль
612	powder	порошок
612	collect	собираться, собирать
612	face powder	пудра для лица
612	meeting	собрание
612	football match	футбольный матч
612	Red Cross	Красный Крест
613	furniture	мебель
613	furnish	обставлять мебелью

613	available	доступный
613	human being	человек
613	artificial	искусственный
614	kiss	целовать
614	rush	устремляться, напряженный (the rush hour - час-пик)
614	hero	герой

LESSON 114

616	dish	блюдо
616	serve	подавать
616	to be for (or against) something	быть за что-то (или против чего-то)
616	arms	оружие
616	fox	лисица
616	fox hunting	охота на лис
617	seize	схватить
617	handbag	сумочка
617	break out	вспыхнуть, разразиться
617	wage	оплата труда
617	salary	оклад, зарплата
617	payment	платеж
617	profession	профессия
617	non - professional	непрофессиональный
617	steady	постоянный, твердый
617	seasonal	сезонный
617	seaside	морское побережье
617	painter	художник
617	pianist	пианист
617	surgeon	хирург
618	leaf	лист
618	loaf	буханка
618	shelf	полка
618	cliff	утес
618	deer	олень
618	wood	лес
619	mention	упоминать
619	tell off	отчитывать
619	partner	партнер
619	insist	настаивать
620	board	доска, совет (директоров), правление, питание
620	floorboard	половица
620	noticeboard	доска объявлений
620	blackboard	школьная доска
620	deck	палуба
620	port	порт
620	director	директор

LESSON 115

622	timetable	расписание
622	schedule	расписание
622	account	перечень, рассказ, счет, учет
623	greedy	жадный
623	satisfied	удовлетворенный
623	crop	сельскохозяйственная культура
623	differ	отличаться
623	private	частный
624	what	который, что
624	whom	кто, кого
626	whose	чей
626	search	искать, обыскивать

Russian vocabulary

626 support ....поддерживать
627 religious ....религиозный

LESSON 116

628 declare............. заявлять, объявлять, оглашать
628 red-handed.................................... с поличным
628 innocent...невиновный
628 upper..высший
628 middle..средний
628 working..рабочий
628 class .... класс
628 society ....общество
628 aristocracy .... аристократия
628 industrialist .... промышленник
628 case................................... регистр (клавиатуры)
628 lower..нижний
629 raise........... поднимать, растить, выращивать,
воздвигать
629 to be excused ....получить разрешение,
....быть отпущенным
629 monument ....монумент, памятник
629 honour .... честь
629 statue .... статуя
630 transitive ....переходный
631 respect... уважение
631 scorn...презрение
631 worthy ....достойный
631 term .... четверть/ семестр
631 worship ....поклоняться
632 cattle............................. крупный рогатый скот
632 cowboy ....ковбой
632 harvest... урожай
632 mother-in-law.......................теща, свекровь
632 father-in-law......................тесть, свекор
632 rail...рельс
632 railing...........................ограждение, перила
632 run ....двигаться
632 protection..защита
632 balcony .... балкон

LESSON 117

634 knowledge .... знание
634 progress ....прогресс
634 item..предмет
634 encyclopedia .... энциклопедия
635 mass... масса
635 advantage...................................преимущество
635 disadvantage .... недостаток
635 mass – production....... массовое производство
635 production..............................производство
635 product ....продукт
635 identical .... идентичный
635 quality ....качество
635 pick up .... поднимать, заезжать, подцепить
635 date .... свидание
635 vocabulary ....лексикон, словарный запас
636 prevent ....предотвращать
636 drum ....барабан, барабанить,
.........................циллиндрический контейнер
636 harbour ....гавань
636 port ....порт
637 nosey..любопытный
637 masculine...............................мужской род
637 feminine..................................... женский род
637 god ....бог
637 goddess ....богиня
637 prince ....принц
637 princess ....принцесса
638 nephew ....племянник

638 niece..племянница
638 landlord.............домовладелец, арендодатель,
....землевладелец
638 landlady........................... домовладелица
638 widower ....вдовец
638 widow .... вдова
638 event .... событие
638 eventful ....насыщенный событиями
638 uneventful.......... без особенных происшествий,
........................событий; непримечательный
638 concern... касаться
639 celebrate ....праздновать
639 celebration................................ празднование
639 New Year's Eve.................... канун Нового Года
639 up to date ....актуальный, действительный
639 out of date ....просроченный
639 essential ....необходимый, важный

LESSON 118

640 article ....артикль
641 countable................................исчисляемый
641 uncountable...........................неисчисляемый
642 worm ....червь
642 silkworm .... шелковичный червь
642 silk ....шелк
642 limb ....конечность
642 poison...яд
643 cave ....пещера
643 bat ....летучая мышь
643 deserve...заслуживать
643 frequent (verb)..................................посещать
643 frequent (adjective)............................ частый
643 frequently (adverb) ....часто
644 attract ....привлекать
644 attention...внимание
644 attraction.....................достопримечательность
644 attractive ....привлекательный
644 good-looking.................................симпатичный
644 the rest ....остальные
644 miserable.......................... жалкий, мерзкий
645 emotion...эмоция
645 emotional..................................эмоциональный

LESSON 119

646 firstly .... во-первых
646 secondly ....во-вторых
646 head teacher .... директор школы
646 study ....кабинет
647 vote...голосовать
647 nurse ....ухаживать за больным, няньчить
647 nursery ....детский сад
647 unemployment............................безработица
647 take off ....взлетать
647 land...приземляться
647 seat belt.....................ремень безопасности
648 practice ....практика
648 theory ....теория
648 practical .... дельный, практичный
648 take into account ....принимать во внимание
648 set up...организовать
649 nature ....натура
649 human nature .... человеческая натура
650 compete..соревноваться
650 competition .... соревнование
650 energy ....энергия
650 efficient ....эффективный
650 suit .... идти, подходить
650 suitable .... подходящий
651 effect.. последствия, воздействие, впечатление

651 perfect ....совершенный
651 to go up to ....подходить к
651 sunshine ....солнечный свет

LESSON 120

653 polish..начищать
653 ability .... способность
653 expense...расход
653 postpone.............откладывать на другое время
654 stress...стресс
654 stressful...напряженный
654 afterwards....................................впоследствии
654 first of all..прежде всего
654 attend .... посещать, обслуживать,
.....................................быть внимательным
654 shopkeeper........................ владелец магазина
655 move ....трогать, волновать;
.... вызывать (какие-л. чувства, эмоции)
655 tear ....слеза
655 pass .... передавать
656 spoil - spoilt - spoilt...
...........................портить - портил - испортил
656 discipline..дисциплина
656 hunger ....голод
656 share ....делиться, делить, акция

LESSON 121

659 association .... ассоциация
659 automobile............................автомобильный
659 disturb..беспокоить
659 concentrate...........................концентрироваться
659 courage .... смелость
659 virtue ....добродетель
660 loyal..верный, преданный
660 loyalty..верность
660 companion.. спутник
660 spirit.........дух, душа, настроение, алкогольный
напиток
660 spiritual..духовный
660 evil...злой
661 flow...течь, поток
661 festival .... фестиваль
661 feast..пир
661 dare ....осмелиться, сметь
661 challenge.................................бросать вызов
662 bring up ....воспитывать
662 solve...решать
662 calculator ....калькулятор
663 fix...................скрепить, назначить, повесить
663 hammer ....молоток
663 nail ....гвоздь
663 fingernail...ноготь
663 criticize ....критиковать

LESSON 122

665 yard ....двор
665 courtyard ....двор
665 enclose .... огораживать
665 space ....пространство
665 amuse............................веселить, развлекать
665 comic .... комичный
665 pass (the time).................... проводить (время)
665 cards...карты
665 waiting room .... приемная
665 amusement.....................................развлечение
666 hobby ....хобби
666 photography ....фотография
666 order ....порядок
666 pack...................................собирать (чемодан)

666 packed..переполненный
666 suitcase .... чемодан
666 shorts..шорты
666 T-shirt...футболка
667 thorn ....шип
667 rose ....роза
667 afford ....позволять себе
667 agreement ....соглашение
667 basket ....корзина
667 trolley...тележка
667 nut...орех
668 regarding .... относительно
668 material..материал
668 duvet.........................стеганое пуховое одеяло
668 cotton ....хлопок
668 leather ....кожа
668 convenience .... удобство, удобства
668 convenient..удобный
668 inconvenient ....неудобный
668 inconvenience ....неудобство
668 dining room.................................столовая
668 sensitive ....чувствительный, чуткий,
....восприимчивый
668 offend ....обидеть
668 criticism ....критика
668 thermometer..термометр
669 sensible .... разумный
669 reasonable...разумный
670 shopping centre........................торговый центр
670 balance. балансировать, сходиться (о цифрах),
....остаток
670 add up ....прибавлять
670 bind - bound - bound ....
.............................связывать - связал - связал

LESSON 123

673 note ....записка, замечать, нота
673 note down.....................................записывать
673 take notes................................... вести заметки
673 notebook................................ записная книжка
673 banknote....................................банкнота
673 key ....клавиша
673 keyboard...клавиатура
674 armour .... доспехи
674 spread .... распространять(ся)
674 all over.....................................по всему
674 fascinated.......................................пораженный
674 scene ....место
674 murderer...убийца
674 evidence .... улика, доказательство
675 i.e. = id est = that is ....т.е. = то есть
675 at first...вначале
675 accustomed .... привычный

LESSON 124

678 benefit..польза
678 sake ....ради
678 give up.................................прекращать
678 mixed up .... перепутанный
678 humour ....юмор
679 dress...одежда
679 master ....мастер, овладевать, усваивать
679 masterpiece......................................шедевр
679 so..........................поэтому, чтобы, итак
679 so that...................................так, чтобы
679 so as to............................... для того, чтобы
679 and so on.......................................и так далее
679 so many.....................................так много
679 so far .... до сих пор

LESSON 125

LESSON 126

Slovak Vocabulary

LESSON 112

603	joke	žartovať, vtip
603	pretend	predstierať
603	envelope	obálka
603	stamp	známka
603	leave out	vynechať
603	postcode	smerovacie číslo
604	naturally	prirodzene
604	recent	nedávny
604	so-so	obstojný, priemerný
604	mate	kamarát, kamoš
604	housemate	spolubývajúci (v dome)
604	flatmate	spolubývajúci (v byte)
604	classmate	spolužiak
604	workmate	kolega
605	to look forward to	tešiť sa na niečo
605	let me see	počkaj chvíľku
606	chance	šanca
606	dismiss	prepustiť
606	jungle	džungľa
606	fifty-fifty	päťdesiat na päťdesiat
606	take a chance	riskovať
606	whistle	pískať
606	hunt	poľovať
607	deed	skutok
607	grease	mazadlo
607	scissors	nožnice
607	take control	prevziať kontrolu
607	lose control	stratiť kontrolu
607	due	splatný, povinný
607	due to	kvôli, z dôvodu
608	grandmother	stará mama
608	grandfather	starý otec
608	great-grandmother	prastará mama
608	great-grandfather	prastarý otec
608	mostly	väčšinou
608	totally	úplne
609	sentence	veta

LESSON 113

610	discuss	diskutovať, rozprávať sa
610	discussion	diskusia
610	argue	hádať sa
610	argument	hádka
610	quarrel	ostro sa hádať
610	anger	hnev
610	reason	dôvod
611	regular	obyčajný, pravidelný
611	do something about	urobiť niečo s
611	blow up	vyhodiť do povetria
612	dust	prach
612	powder	prášok
612	collect	zbierať, zhromaždiť
612	face powder	púder na tvár
612	meeting	stretnutie, zhromaždenie
612	football match	futbalový zápas
612	Red Cross	Červený kríž
613	furniture	nábytok
613	furnish	zariadiť
613	available	dostupný
613	human being	ľudský tvor
613	artificial	umelý

614	kiss	bozk, pobozkať
614	rush	ponáhľať sa, (r.hour špička)
614	hero	hrdina

LESSON 114

616	dish	misa, jedlo
616	serve	podávať, servírovať
616	to be for (or against) something	byť za (alebo proti) niečomu
616	arms	zbrane
616	fox	líška
616	fox hunting	hon na líšku
617	seize	uchmatnúť
617	handbag	kabelka
617	break out	vypuknúť
617	wage	mzda (vypočítaná podľa odpracovaných hodín)
617	salary	mzda (stály plat, pevná čiastka)
617	payment	výplata, platba
617	profession	profesia
617	non - professional	neprofesionálny
617	steady	pevný, stály
617	seasonal	sezónny
617	seaside	prímorský
617	painter	maliar
617	pianist	klavirista
617	surgeon	chirurg
618	leaf	list
618	loaf	bochník, peceň
618	shelf	polica
618	cliff	útes
618	deer	jeleň, jelene
618	wood	les
619	mention	spomenúť
619	tell off	vyhrešiť
619	partner	partner
619	insist	naliehať, trvať na niečom
620	board	doska, nalodiť sa, nastúpiť do..
620	floorboard	podlahová doska
620	noticeboard	nástenka
620	blackboard	tabuľa
620	deck	paluba
620	port	prístav
620	director	riaditeľ (board of directors - predstavenstvo)

LESSON 115

622	timetable	časový harmonogram, cestovný poriadok
622	schedule	program, rozvrh
622	account	správa, účet, evidencia
623	greedy	chamtivý, nenásytný
623	satisfied	spokojný
623	crop	plodina, úroda
623	differ	líšiť sa
623	private	súkromný
624	what	čo
624	whom	ktorého
626	whose	ktorého (namiesto privlastňovacieho zámena)
626	search	pátrať, hľadať
626	support	podopierať, podporovať

.... (byť fanúšikom)
627 religious ....náboženský

LESSON 116

628 declare...vyhlásiť
628 red-handed .... pri čine
628 innocent...nevinný
628 upper...vyšší
628 middle... stredný
628 working...pracujúci
628 class...trieda
628 society ....spoločnosť
628 aristocracy ....aristokracia
628 industrialist ....priemyselník
628 case...prípad
628 lower...nižší
629 raise........................... zdvihnúť, vztýčiť, vychovať
629 to be excused ....byť ospravedlnený
629 monument .... pamätník, pomník
629 honour....................................česť, pamiatka
629 statue...socha
630 transitive ....tranzitívny, prechodný
631 respect..rešpekt
631 scorn...pohŕdanie
631 worthy...............................byť hodný niečoho
631 term .... semester
631 worship.....................vykonať pobožnosť
632 cattle...dobytok
632 cowboy ....pastier dobytka
632 harvest...................................... žatva, úroda
632 mother-in-law................................ svokra
632 father-in-law.................................. svokor
632 rail..koľaj
632 railing...zábradlie
632 run ....premávať, fungovať
632 protection...ochrana
632 balcony..balkón

LESSON 117

634 knowledge ....vedomosť, znalosť
634 progress ....pokrok
634 item...položka
634 encyclopedia ....encyklopédia
635 mass.. masa
635 advantage... výhoda
635 disadvantage ....nevýhoda
635 mass – production ....masová výroba
635 production..výroba
635 product .... výrobok
635 identical .... rovnaký
635 quality...kvalita
635 pick up.................zdvihnúť, vyzdvihnúť niekoho,
.... pochytiť (náhodne sa naučiť)
635 date .... rande, schôdzka
635 vocabulary ....slovná zásoba
636 prevent ....predísť
636 drum .... bubnovať,
.................kovový sud, bubon (hudobný nástroj)
636 harbour .... prístav (krytý)
636 port ....prístav
637 nosey...zvedavý, všetečný
637 masculine ....mužský (rod)
637 feminine .... ženský (rod)
637 god ....boh
637 goddess .... bohyňa
637 prince.. princ
637 princess..princezná
638 nephew..synovec
638 niece...neter

638 landlord.. majiteľ domu
638 landlady .... majiteľka domu
638 widower ....vdovec
638 widow .... vdova
638 event.. udalosť
638 eventful.....................rušný (bohatý na udalosti)
638 uneventful..........................chudobný na udalosti
638 concern... týkať sa
639 celebrate..oslavovať
639 celebration...oslava
639 New Year's Eve....................................Silvester
639 up to date ....aktuálny, platný
639 out of date ....zastaraný, po záruke
639 essential ....dôležitý, základný

LESSON 118

640 article......................................člen (gramatický)
641 countable.. počítateľný
641 uncountable................................... nepočítateľný
642 worm... červ
642 silkworm .... priadka morušová
642 silk ....hodváb
642 limb..končatina
642 poison...jed
643 cave..jaskyňa
643 bat ....netopier
643 deserve.. zaslúžiť si
643 frequent (verb)...............................navštevovať
643 frequent (adjective)....................................častý
643 frequently (adverb) .... často
644 attract ....pritiahnuť
644 attention... atrakcia
644 attraction................... atraktívny, príťažlivý
644 attractive..pozornosť
644 good-looking..........................pekný, vzhľadný
644 the rest ....zvyšok
644 miserable.................. mizerný, biedny, chudobný
645 emotion.. emócia
645 emotional.. dojatý

LESSON 119

646 firstly...poprvé
646 secondly ....po druhé
646 head teacher ....riaditeľ školy
646 study... kabinet
647 vote.. voliť
647 nurse ...... sať, opatrovať (chorého človeka, dieťa)
647 nursery .... jasle, škôlka
647 unemployment.........................nezamestnanosť
647 take off...vzlietnuť
647 land...pristáť
647 seat belt..bezpečnostný pás
648 practice...prax
648 theory ....teória
648 practical...praktický
648 take into account ....vziať do úvahy
648 set up..založiť
649 nature ....povaha
649 human nature ....ľudská povaha
650 compete..súťažiť
650 competition...súťaž
650 energy ....energia
650 efficient .... efektívny, výkonný
650 suit...............................hodiť sa, vyhovovať
650 suitable .... vhodný
651 effect............................ efekt, účinok, následok
651 perfect ....úplný
651 to go up to ....podísť k

LESSON 120

651	sunshine	slnešno
653	polish	leštiť
653	ability	schopnosť
653	expense	výdavok
653	postpone	preložiť
654	stress	stres
654	stressful	stresujúci
654	afterwards	potom
654	first of all	predovšetkým
654	attend	navštevovať, obsluhovať, dávať pozor
654	shopkeeper	obchodník, majiteľ obchodu
655	move	dojať, (moving - dojemný)
655	tear	slza
655	pass	podať
656	spoil - spoilt - spoilt	rozmaznať (základný tvar)
		– rozmaznať (minulý čas)
		– rozmaznať (minulé príčastie)
656	discipline	disciplína
656	hunger	hlad
656	share	podeliť sa, zdieľať, podiel (obchodný)

LESSON 121

659	association	asociácia, združenie
659	automobile	automobilový
659	disturb	rušiť
659	concentrate	sústrediť sa
659	courage	odvaha
659	virtue	cnosť
660	loyal	oddaný
660	loyalty	oddanosť
660	companion	spoločník
660	spirit	prístup, duša, duch, nadšenie, destilát
660	spiritual	duchovný
660	evil	zlý
661	flow	tiecť, prúdiť
661	festival	festival
661	feast	hostina
661	dare	odvážiť sa
661	challenge	výzva
662	bring up	vyrastať, vychovávať
662	solve	riešiť
662	calculator	kalkulačka
663	fix	upevniť, pripevniť, plánovať
663	hammer	kladivo
663	nail	klinec
663	fingernail	necht
663	criticize	kritizovať

LESSON 122

665	yard	dvor
665	courtyard	nádvorie
665	enclose	obkolesiť
665	space	priestor
665	amuse	zabávať
665	comic	komický
665	pass (the time)	plynúť
665	cards	karty
665	waiting room	čakáreň
665	amusement	zábava, rozptýlenie
666	hobby	hobby, koníček
666	photography	fotografovanie
666	order	poradie
666	pack	baliť, zabaliť
666	packed	plný, preplnený
666	suitcase	kufor
666	shorts	šortky
666	T-shirt	tričko

667	thorn	tŕň
667	rose	ruža
667	afford	dovoliť si
667	agreement	dohoda
667	basket	košík
667	trolley	vozík
667	nut	orech
668	regarding	týkajúci sa
668	material	materiál
668	duvet	perina
668	cotton	bavlna
668	leather	koža
668	convenience	výhoda, vymoženosť
668	convenient	vyhovujúci, vhodný
668	inconvenient	nepohodlie
668	inconvenience	nevyhovujúci
668	dining room	jedáleň
668	sensitive	jemný, citlivý
668	offend	uraziť
668	criticism	kritika
668	thermometer	teplomer
669	sensible	praktický, rozumný
669	reasonable	rozumný
670	shopping centre	nákupné centrum
670	balance	vážiť, vyrovnaný, zostatok
670	add up	spočítať
670	bind - bound - bound	zaviazať (základný tvar)
		– zaviazať (minulý čas)
		– zaviazať (minulé príčastie)

LESSON 123

673	note	poznámka, tón, všimnúť si, farba hlasu
673	note down	poznačiť si
673	take notes	robiť si poznámky
673	notebook	zošit
673	banknote	bankovka
673	key	kláves
673	keyboard	klávesnica
674	armour	brnenie
674	spread	šíriť sa
674	all over	všade
674	fascinated	fascinovaný
674	scene	miesto, scéna
674	murderer	vrah
674	evidence	dôkaz
675	i.e. = id est = that is	i.e. = id est = tzn.
675	at first	najskôr
675	accustomed	zvyknutý

LESSON 124

678	benefit	úžitok, osoh
678	sake	kvôli, v záujme
678	give up	prestať
678	mixed up	popletený, pomiešaný
678	humour	humor
679	dress	oblečenie
679	master	majster, osvojiť si
679	masterpiece	majstrovské dielo
679	so	tak
679	so that	aby
679	so as to	aby
679	and so on	a tak ďalej
679	so many	tak veľa
679	so far	zatiaľ
679	so far as I know	pokiaľ viem
681	praise	chváliť, pochvala
681	loan	pôžička
681	furthermore	okrem toho, navyše
681	moreover	okrem toho, navyše

682 toe ....palec (na nohe)
682 personally .... osobne
682 conscious .... vedomý
682 unconscious ....nevedomí, v bezvedomí
682 self-conscious.................. rozpačitý, v rozpakoch
682 patient... pacient
682 injection ....injekcia
682 gathering ....stretnutie, zhromaždenie
683 split..............................štiepať, roztrhnúť, rozdeliť
683 axe... sekera
683 equally... rovnako

LESSON 125

684 Alps ....Alpy
684 Andes ....Andy
684 Himalayas..Himaláje
684 Netherlands ....Holandsko
685 present (noun +adj) ....prítomnosť,
.... darček, prítomný
685 present (verb) ....predstaviť, uviesť, venovať
686 swear - swore - sworn .... hrešiť, nadávať
.... (základný tvar)
............................– hrešiť, nadávať (minulý čas)
.....................– hrešiť, nadávať (minulé príčastie)
687 lazy ....lenivý
687 idle...lenivý (o človeku)
687 play...................................... divadelná hra
687 scene... scéna
688 verse... verš
688 chorus...refrén
688 pray .... modliť sa
688 prayer .... modlitba
688 combine.................................spájať, kombinovať
689 heads..........................lícna strana mince (hlava)
689 tails... rub mince

LESSON 126

690 extend.......................................rozšíriť, natiahnuť
690 as far as... pokiaľ, až po
691 trust ....dôvera, sporiaci účet
691 dependent .... závislý
691 independent... nezávislý
692 punctual...................................presný, dochvíľny
692 row...veslovať
692 oar ....veslo
692 wish ....želať si
693 ideal..teoretický
693 theoretical...teoretický
693 actual...skutočný
693 actually .... v skutočnosti
694 check... skontrolovať
694 change..drobné
694 log..poleno
694 fireplace .... kozub
694 common sense .... zdravý rozum
695 tool... nástroj
695 bean ....fazuľa

Spanish Vocabulary

LESSON 112

603 joke..........bromear, hacer gracias, broma, chiste
603 pretend ....pretender, fingir
603 envelope...sobre
603 stamp........................sellar, poner un sello, sello
603 leave out....................................omitir, no incluir
603 postcode..código postal
604 naturally.....de modo/forma natural, naturalmente
604 recent .... reciente
604 so-so.......................así así, ni fu ni fa, mediocre
604 mate ....amigo/a (informal)
604 housemate................... compañero/a de casa
604 flatmate........................... compañero/a de piso
604 classmate ....compañero/a de clase
604 workmate....................compañero/a de trabajo
605 to look forward to............ desear, tener ganas de
605 let me see...............................a ver, déjame ver,
....déjame que piense
606 chance..oportunidad
606 dismiss ....despedir
606 jungle...selva, jungla
606 fifty-fifty ....un 50% de posibilidades,
....mitad y mitad
606 take a chance...intentar
606 whistle .... silbar
606 hunt .... cazar
607 deed ....hecho, acción
607 grease ....grasa
607 scissors .... tijeras
607 take control...................................tomar control
607 lose control ....perder control
607 due ....debido/a/os/as, requerido/a/os/as,
....previsto/a/os/as
607 due to .... debido a
608 grandmother..abuela
608 grandfather..abuelo
608 great-grandmother................................bisabuela
608 great-grandfather................................bisabuelo
608 mostly... en su mayoría
608 totally.......................totalmente, completamente
609 sentence.. sentenciar

LESSON 113

610 discuss ....hablar, debatir
610 discussion..debate
610 argue ....discutir, argumentar
610 argument ....discusión, argumento
610 quarrel ....reñir, riña
610 anger ....enfado
610 reason ....razonar, argumentar
611 regular ....normal, habitual, frecuente
611 do something about...............hacer algo por/para
611 blow up...hacer volar
612 dust..........................polvo (de origan natural)
612 powder...........................polvo (manufacturado)
612 collect .... acumular, recoger,
....coleccionar, reunirse
612 face powder..........................polvos para la cara
612 meeting..reunión
612 football match ....partido de fútbol
612 Red Cross ....Cruz Roja
613 furniture ....muebles, mobiliario

613 furnish..amueblar
613 available ....disponible, libre
613 human being................................ser humano
613 artificial ....artificial/es
614 kiss ....besar, beso
614 rush ....darse prisa, apresurarse
614 hero ....héroe

LESSON 114

616 dish.....................fuente (para servir comida)
616 serve..servir
616 to be for (or against) something ....estar a favor
......................................(o en contra) de algo
616 arms ....armas
616 fox...zorro
616 fox hunting....................................caza del zorro
617 seize...................agarrar, arrebatar, dar un tirón
617 handbag ....bolso (de mano)
617 break out ....estallar (una guerra)
617 wage...................................paga, sueldo, salario
617 salary....................salario, sueldo, remuneración
617 payment...pago
617 profession ....profesión
617 non - professional.........................no profesional
617 steady...............fijo/a/os/as, firme/s, constante/s
617 seasonal..estacional
617 seaside...costero/a/os/as
617 painter ....pintor/a
617 pianist ....pianista
617 surgeon ....cirujano/a
618 leaf.. hoja
618 loaf.....................pan, barra de pan, hogaza
618 shelf... estante, balda
618 cliff...acantilado
618 deer .... ciervo
618 wood...bosque
619 mention ....mencionar
619 tell off.......... regañar, reñir (una persona a otra/s)
619 partner ....socio/a
619 insist ....insistir
620 board .... tabla, tablón
620 floorboard ....tabla del suelo
620 noticeboard............tablero/tablón m de anuncios
620 blackboard..............................pizarra, encerado
620 deck... cubierta
620 port ....puerto
620 director ....directivo/a, director/a

LESSON 115

622 timetable..horario
622 schedule............. programa o calendario de algo
622 account.......... explicación, cuenta (bancaria,etc),
.... to keep an account of = llevar la cuenta de
623 greedy ....codicioso/a/os/as, avaricioso/a/os/as
623 satisfied .... satisfecho/a/os/as
623 crop ....cultivo
623 differ ....diferir, diferenciarse
623 private...privado/a/os/as
623 what... lo que
624 whom...............al/a la/a los/a las que, a quien/es,
.... etc dependiendo de la frase y de si le
acompaña una preposición como 'with', 'by', etc.

..... 'whom' puede sustituir a 'who', sobre todo en
...............lenguaje formal, cuando 'who' no es el
.... ujeto de la frase
626 whose..cuyo/a/os/as
626 search.................................... buscar, registrar
626 support .... sostener, apoyar
627 religious ....religioso/a/os/as

LESSON 116

628 declare................................ declarar, manifestar
628 red-handed .... con las manos en la masa
628 innocent...inocente/s
628 upper................................superior/es, de arriba
.... (upper class = clase alta,
...................uppercase letter = letra mayúscula)
628 middle...medio/a/os/as
.... (middle class = clase media)
628 working ....trabajador/a/os/as
.... (working class = clase trabajadora)
628 class ....clase
628 society ....sociedad
628 aristocracy ....aristocracia
628 industrialist .... industrial/es (nombre)
628 case... tipo de letra
628 lower.................................... inferior/es, de abajo
....(lower class = clase baja,
.... lowercase letter = letra minúscula)
629 raise.................................levantar, criar, erigir
629 to be excused .... pedir/dar permiso para salir
629 monument .... monumento
629 honour ....honor
629 statue... estatua
630 transitive....................................transitivo/a/os/as
631 respect...respeto
631 scorn..............................despreció, menosprecio
631 worthy..........digno/a/os/as, merecedor/a/os/as
.... (de algo o alguien)
631 term ....trimestre
631 worship ....rendir culto, adorar, venerar
632 cattle.. ganado, reses
632 cowboy ....vaquero (persona)
632 harvest...cosecha
632 mother-in-law..suegra
632 father-in-law....................................suegro
632 rail... riel, raíl
632 railing...reja, verja
632 run ....circular (tren, autobús)
632 protection.. protección
632 balcony ....balcón

LESSON 117

634 knowledge ....conocimiento
634 progress ....progreso
634 item........items of' se usa para indicar el plural de
..............algunos nombres que carecen de plural
..........en inglés, por ejemplo: 5 items of furniture
.... = 5 muebles
634 encyclopedia ....enciclopedia
635 mass.. masa
635 advantage.. ventaja
635 disadvantage.....................................desventaja
635 mass – production ....producción en masa
635 production.. producción
635 product ....producto
635 identical ....idéntico/a/os/as
635 quality...calidad
636 pick up............levantar, recoger, pasar a buscar,
....aprender
636 date .... cita

636 vocabulary ....vocabulario
636 prevent .... prevenir, evitar
636 drum ....tamborilear con los dedos,
...........................bidón metálico, tambor, batería
636 harbour..puerto
636 port...puerto
637 nosey......... entrometido/a/os/as, cotilla (adjetivo)
637 masculine .... masculino/a/os/as
637 feminine....................................femenino/a/os/as
637 god .... dios
637 goddess... diosa
637 prince... príncipe
637 princess .... princesa
638 nephew... sobrino
638 niece.. sobrina
638 landlord.. casero
638 landlady.. casera
638 widower .... viudo
638 widow .... viuda
638 event...acontecimiento
638 eventful.............lleno/a/os/as de acontecimientos
638 uneventful.................... sin acontecimientos
638 concern... concernir
639 celebrate...celebrar
639 celebration.....................................celebración
639 New Year's Eve .... Nochevieja,
.... Noche de Fin de Año
639 up to date .... de moda, al día,
....actualizado/a/os/as
639 out of date ....pasado/a/os/as de moda,
....caducado/a/os/as
639 essential ....esencial/es

LESSON 118

640 article.. artículo
641 countable..contables
641 uncountable................................... incontables
642 worm .... gusano
642 silkworm .... gusano de seda
642 silk .... seda
642 limb................................extremidad (del cuerpo)
642 poison... veneno
643 cave.. cueva
643 bat .... murciélago
643 deserve...merecer(se)
643 frequent (verb)...................................frecuentar
643 frequent (adjective)............................. frecuente/s
643 frequently (adverb) ....con frecuencia,
....frecuentemente
643 accent... acento
644 attract ....atraer
644 attraction.. atracción
644 attractive..atractivo/a/os/as
644 attention.. atención
644 good-looking...... guapo/a/os/as, atractivo/a/os/as
644 the rest .... el resto
644 miserable.......................triste/s, abatido/a/os/as,
..........con el ánimo por los suelos, deprimente/s
645 emotion.. emoción
645 emotional..emocional

LESSON 119

646 firstly ....primero, en primer lugar
646 secondly .... segundo, en segundo lugar
646 head teacher ....director/a de colegio
646 study.. estudio
647 vote...votar
647 nurse .... cuidar, atender
647 nursery ....guardería

647 unemployment .... paro, desempleo
647 take off .... despegar (un avión)
647 land .... aterrizar (un avión)
647 seat belt .... cinturón de seguridad
648 practice .... práctica
648 theory .... teoría
648 practical .... práctico/a/os/as
648 take into account .... tener en cuenta
648 set up .... montar, crear o establecer
649 nature .... naturaleza
649 human nature .... naturaleza humana
650 compete .... competir
650 competition .... competición
650 energy .... energía
650 efficient .... eficiente/s
650 suit .... sentar bien (ropa), convenir
650 suitable ...... apropiado/a/os/as, adecuado/a/os/as
651 effect .... efecto
651 perfect .... total, perfecto
651 to go up to .... acercarse a
651 sunshine .... sol

LESSON 120

653 polish .... abrillantar
653 ability .... capacidad, aptitud
653 expense .... gasto
653 postpone .... aplazar, posponer
654 stress .... estrés, tensión
654 stressful .... estresante
654 afterwards .... después
654 first of all .... en primer lugar, antes que nada
654 attend .... asistir, atender
654 shopkeeper .... tendero/a, comerciante
655 move .... conmover, emocionar
655 tear .... lágrima
655 pass .... pasarle
656 spoil – spoilt – spoilt .... estropear, arruinar,
.... echar a perder, mimar demasiado, consentir
656 discipline .... desciplina
656 hunger .... hambre
656 share .... compartir, participación, acción

LESSON 121

659 association .... asociación
659 automobile .... automóvil
659 disturb .... molestar
659 concentrate .... concentrar(se)
659 courage .... valor, coraje
659 virtue .... virtud
660 loyal .... leal/es
660 loyalty .... lealtad
660 companion .... compañero/a
660 spirit .... espíritu, ánimo, bebida alcohólica
660 spiritual .... espiritual/es
660 evil .... maligno/a/os/as
661 flow .... fluir
661 festival .... festival
661 feast .... banquete, festín
661 dare .... atreverse, retar,
.... desafiar a alguien a hacer algo
661 challenge .... retar, desafiar
662 bring up .... criar
662 solve .... resolver
662 calculator .... calculadora
663 fix .... sujetar, asegurar, concertar (una cita)
663 hammer .... martillo
663 nail .... clavo
663 fingernail .... uña
663 criticize .... criticar

LESSON 122

665 yard .... yarda
665 courtyard .... patio
665 enclose .... rodear, cercar
665 space .... espacio
665 amuse .... divertir(se)
665 comic .... cómico/a/os/as
665 pass (the time) .... pasar (el tiempo)
665 cards .... cartas (de jugar)
665 waiting room .... sala de espera
665 amusement .... distracción, entretenimiento
666 hobby .... afición, pasatiempo
666 photography .... fotografía
666 order .... orden
666 pack .... hacer la maleta
666 packed .... lleno, repleto
666 suitcase .... maleta
666 shorts .... shorts, pantalones cortos
666 T-shirt .... camiseta
667 thorn .... pincho
667 rose .... rosa
667 afford .... permitirse
667 agreement .... acuerdo
667 basket .... cesta
667 trolley .... carrito
667 nut .... fruto seco
668 regarding .... en lo que concierne a,
.... en lo que se refiere a, (con) respecto a
668 material .... material
668 duvet .... edredón
668 cotton .... algodón
668 leather .... cuero, piel
668 convenience .... conveniencia, comodidad
668 convenient .... conveniente/s, cómodo/a/os/as
668 inconvenience .... inconveniencia, incomodidad
668 inconvenient .... inconveniente/s,
.... incómodo/a/os/as
668 dining room .... comedor
668 sensitive .... sensible/s, delicado/a/os/as
668 offend .... ofender
668 criticism .... crítica
668 thermometer .... termómetro
669 sensible .... sensato/a/os/as, prudente/s
669 reasonable .... razonable/s
670 shopping centre .... centro comercial
670 balance .... mantener/sostener en equilibrio,
.... equilibrar, balance, resto
670 add up .... sumar
670 bind – bound – bound .... atar, vendar
.... (una herida), encuadernar (un libro),
.... comprometerse (con una promesa)

LESSON 123

673 note .... notar, nota, apunte
673 note down .... tomar nota, anotar, apuntar
673 take notes .... tomar notas/apuntes
673 notebook .... cuaderno
673 banknote .... billete
673 key .... tecla (de piano, de teclado)
673 keyboard .... teclado
674 armour .... armadura
674 spread .... extender(se)
674 all over .... por todo/a/os/as
674 fascinated .... fascinado/a/os/as
674 scene .... escena
674 murderer .... asesino/a/os/as
674 evidence .... pruebas
675 i.e. = id est = that is .... esto es, a saber

Spanish vocabulary

Turkish Vocabulary

LESSON 112

603	joke	şaka/şaka yapmak
603	pretend	gibi davranmak
603	envelope	zarf
603	stamp	pul/mühür/damgalamak
603	leave out	eklemeyi unutmak
603	postcode	posta kodu
604	naturally	doğal olarak
604	recent	son zamanlarda
604	so-so	şöyle böyle
604	mate	arkadaş
604	housemate	ev arkadaşı
604	flatmate	ev arkadaşı
604	classmate	sınıf arkadaşı
604	workmate	iş arkadaşı
605	to look forward to	dört gözle beklemek
605	let me see	bir düşüneyim
606	chance	şans
606	dismiss	kovmak
606	jungle	orman
606	fifty-fifty	yarı yarıya
606	take a chance	denemek/riske girmek
606	whistle	ıslık çalmak
606	hunt	avlamak
607	deed	yapılan iş/eylem
607	grease	gres yağı
607	scissors	makas
607	take control	kontrolü ele almak
607	lose control	kontrolü kaybetmek
607	due	zamanı gelmiş/beklenen/sebebiyle
607	due to	'den dolayı
608	grandmother	büyük anne
608	grandfather	büyük baba
608	great-grandmother	büyük büyük anne
608	great-grandfather	büyük büyük baba
608	mostly	çoğunlukla
608	totally	tamamıyla
609	sentence	cümle

LESSON 113

610	discuss	tartışmak
610	discussion	tartışma
610	argue	münakaşa etmek
610	argument	münakaşa
610	quarrel	ağız kavgası yapmak
610	anger	sinir
610	reason	sebep
611	regular	düzenli
611	do something about	hakkında bir şeyler yapmak
611	blow up	havaya uçurmak
612	dust	toz
612	powder	pudra/toz
612	collect	toplamak
612	face powder	yüz pudrası
612	meeting	toplantı
612	football match	futbol maçı
612	Red Cross	Kızıl Haç
613	furniture	mobilya
613	furnish	mobilya döşemek
613	available	mümkün/müsait
613	human being	insanoğlu
613	artificial	suni

614	kiss	öpmek
614	rush	acele etmek
614	hero	kahraman

LESSON 114

616	dish	tabak
616	serve	servis etmek
616	to be for (or against) something	bir şeyin lehine (aleyhine) olmak
616	arms	silahlar
616	fox	tilki
616	fox hunting	tilki avı
617	seize	kapmak/gaspetmek
617	handbag	el çantası
617	break out	Patlak vermek/ çıkmak
617	wage	ücret
617	salary	maaş
617	payment	ödeme
617	profession	meslek
617	non - professional	profesyonel olmayan
617	steady	sabit
617	seasonal	sezonluk
617	seaside	deniz kenarı
617	painter	ressam
617	pianist	piyanist
617	surgeon	cerrah
618	leaf	yaprak
618	loaf	ekmek somunu
618	shelf	raf
618	cliff	kayalık
618	deer	geyik
618	wood	ormanlık arazi
619	mention	bahsetmek
619	tell off	azarlamak
619	partner	ortak
619	insist	ısrar etmek
620	boardpano/(vapura/trene/otobüse/uçağa) binmek / yönetim kurulu	
620	floorboard	döşeme tahtası
620	noticeboard	bildirim panosu
620	blackboard	kara tahta
620	deck	güverte
620	port	liman
620	director	yönetici

LESSON 115

622	timetable	zaman çizelgesi
622	schedule	program/plan
622	account	kısa özet / hesap
623	greedy	hırslı
623	satisfied	hoşnut/memnun
623	crop	ekin
623	differ	farklı olmak/farklı düşünmek
623	private	özel
624	what	ne
624	whom	kime
626	whose	kimin
626	search	araştırmak/aramak
626	support	desteklemek
627	religious	dini

LESSON 116

628	declare	beyan etmek/ilan etmek/açıklamak
628	red-handed	suçüstü
628	innocent	masum
628	upper	üst
628	middle	orta
628	working	işçi
628	class	sınıf
628	society	toplum
628	aristocracy	aristokrasi
628	industrialist	sanayici
628	case	(letter) harfin büyük mü küçük mü olduğu
628	lower	alt/düşürmek
629	raise	kaldırmak/yetiştirmek/dikmek
629	to be excused	izinli olmak
629	monument	anıt
629	honour	şeref
629	statue	heykel
630	transitive	geçişli
631	respect	saygı duymak
631	scorn	küçümseme/hor görme
631	worthy	değerli
631	term	dönem
631	worship	ibadet etmek
632	cattle	sığır
632	cowboy	kovboy
632	harvest	hasat
632	mother-in-law	kayın valide
632	father-in-law	kayın peder
632	rail	ray
632	railing	parmaklık
632	run	koşmak
632	protection	koruma
632	balcony	balkon

LESSON 117

634	knowledge	bilgi
634	progress	ilerleme
634	item	parça
634	encyclopedia	ansiklopedi
635	mass	Kitle
635	advantage	avantaj
635	disadvantage	dezavantaj
635	mass – production	Toptan üretim/seri üretim
635	production	üretim
635	product	ürün
635	identical	aynı
635	quality	kalite
635	pick up	almak/(bir şeyi) kaldırmak/kulaktan öğrenmek
635	date	buluşma/flört etmek
635	vocabulary	kelime dağarcığı
636	prevent	önlemek
636	drum	davul/davul çalmak/bidon
636	harbour	gemilerin barındığı yer - liman
636	port	gemilerin yolcu indirip bindirdiği, yük boşaltıp yüklediği yer - liman
637	nosey	meraklı
637	masculine	erkek
637	feminine	dişi
637	god	Tanrı
637	goddess	Tanrıça
637	prince	prens
637	princess	prenses
638	nephew	erkek yeğen
638	niece	kız yeğen
638	landlord	mal sahibi (erkek)
638	landlady	mal sahibi (bayan)

638	widower	dul erkek
638	widow	dul bayan
638	event	olay
638	eventful	olaylarla dolu
638	uneventful	olaysız
638	concern	ilgilendirmek
639	celebrate	kutlamak
639	celebration	kutlama
639	New Year's Eve	Yılbaşı Arifesi
639	up to date	güncel
639	out of date	modası geçmiş/ kullanma tarihi geçmiş
639	essential	elzem/şart

LESSON 118

640	article	isim edatı
641	countable	sayılabilir
641	uncountable	sayılamaz
642	worm	solucan
642	silkworm	ipek böceği
642	silk	ipek
642	limb	uzuv
642	poison	zehir
643	cave	mağara
643	bat	yarasa
643	deserve	hak etmek
643	frequent (verb)	sık sık gitmek (fiil)
643	frequent (adjective)	sık sık tekrarlanan (sıfat)
643	frequently (adverb)	sıklıkla (zarf)
644	attract	dikkatini çekmek
644	attention	dikkat
644	attraction	cazibe
644	attractive	çekici/alımlı
644	good-looking	iyi görünen
644	the rest	geri kalanı
644	miserable	çok kötü/
645	emotion	duygu
645	emotional	duygusal

LESSON 119

646	firstly	ilk olarak
646	secondly	ikinci olarak
646	head teacher	okul müdürü
646	study	çalışma odası
647	vote	oy kullanmak
647	nurse	iyileştirmek/bakıcılık yapmak
647	nursery	ana okulu
647	unemployment	işsizlik
647	take off	uçağın kalkması
647	land	iniş yapmak
647	seat belt	emniyet kemeri
648	practice	deneme
648	theory	teori
648	practical	pratik
648	take into account	dikkate almak
648	set up	kurmak
649	nature	doğa
649	human nature	insan doğası
650	compete	rekabet etmek
650	competition	rekabet
650	energy	enerji
650	efficient	verimli
650	suit	uymak
650	suitable	uygun
651	effect	etki/etki etmek
651	perfect	mükemmel
651	to go up to	birinin yanına gitmek
651	sunshine	güneş ışığı

LESSON 120

653 polish .... cilalamak
653 ability .... beceri
653 expense.. masraf
653 postpone... ertelemek
654 stress.. stres
654 stressful...stresli
654 afterwards... daha sonra
654 first of all .... her şeyden önce
654 attend .... katılmak/hizmet etmek/dinlemek
654 shopkeeper...................................... mağaza sahibi
655 move... hareket etmek
655 tear .... gözyaşı dökmek
655 pass.. vermek
656 spoil - spoilt - spoilt..................... bozmak/şımarık
656 discipline... disiplin
656 hunger .... açlık
656 share .... paylaşmak/pay/hisse

LESSON 121

659 association .... dernek
659 automobile.. otomobil
659 disturb.. rahatsız etmek
659 concentrate............................. konsantre olmak
659 courage .... cesaret
659 virtue.. erdem
660 loyal.. sadık
660 loyalty .... sadakat
660 companion... arkadaş
660 spirit................................ ruh/moral/alkollü içkiler
660 spiritual.. ruhani
660 evil.. kötü /kötülük
661 flow.. akmak
661 festival .... festival
661 feast.. ziyafet
661 dare .... cesaret etmek
661 challenge................................... meydan okumak
662 bring up .... (çocuk) büyütmek
662 solve...çözmek
662 calculator .... hesap makinesi
663 fix.................................... sabitlemek/ayarlamak
663 hammer.. çekiç
663 nail.. çivi
663 fingernail... tırnak
663 criticize .... eleştirmek

LESSON 122

665 yard .... avlu
665 courtyard .... iç bahçe
665 enclose .... çevrelemek
665 space.. yer
665 amuse...................... neşelendirmek/oyalamak
665 comic.. komik
665 pass (the time)...................... (zamanı) geçirmek
665 cards.................................... iskambil kartları
665 waiting room .... bekleme odası
665 amusement.. eğlence
666 hobby.. hobi
666 photography .... fotoğrafçılık
666 order... sıra
666 pack.................... hazırlamak(bavul)/paketlemek
666 packed................................... ağzına kadar dolu
666 suitcase .... valiz
666 shorts.. şort
666 T-shirt.. tişört
667 thorn .... diken
667 rose .... gül
667 afford .... parası yetmek /zaman ayırabilmek

667 agreement .... anlaşma
667 basket.. sepet
667 trolley.................................... süpermarket arabası
667 nut... fındık
668 regarding .... ile ilgili
668 material.. malzeme
668 duvet... yorgan
668 cotton.. pamuk
668 leather ....deri
668 convenienceKolaylık/uygunluk/rahatlık/ elverişlilik
668 convenient.. uygun
668 inconvenient .... zahmetli /uygunsuz
668 inconvenience .... Rahatsızlık/uygunsuzluk
668 dining room.. yemek odası
668 sensitive ....hassas
668 offend .... küstürmek/kırmak
668 criticism.. eleştiri
668 thermometer .... termometre
669 sensible .... mantıklı /akıllı
669 reasonable... makul
670 shopping centre........................ alışveriş merkezi
670 balance.................... dengede tutmak/eşit/kalan
670 add up .... toplamak
670 bind - bound - bound .... bağlamak

LESSON 123

673 note .... not /farketmek/nota
673 note down .... not etmek
673 take notes .... not almak
673 notebook.. defter
673 banknote.. kağıt para
673 key .... tuş
673 keyboard.. klavye
674 armour .... zırh
674 spread .... yayılmak
674 all over .... her yerinde
674 fascinated...büyülenmiş
674 scene.. olay yeri
674 murderer.. katil
674 evidence .... kanıt
675 i.e. = id est = that is .... yani
675 at first... ilk olarak
675 accustomed.. alışkın

LESSON 124

678 benefit............................. Fayda/ kazanç
678 sake... hatır
678 give up.. bırakmak
678 mixed up .... karıştırmak
678 humour .... Mizah
679 dress... elbise
679 master .... usta/ustalaşmak
679 masterpiece.. şaheser
679 so.......................................bu yüzden, böylelikle
679 so that... böylece
679 so as to.. ...'mek amacıyla
679 and so on.. ve benzeri
679 so many... pek çok
679 so far .... bu zamana dek
679 so far as I know .... bildiğim kadarıyla
681 praise....................................... övmek/övgü
681 loan.. kredi
681 furthermore... ayrıca
681 moreover .... dahası
682 toe .... ayak parmağı
682 personally .... şahsen/kişisel olarak
682 conscious .... bilinçli
682 unconscious .... bilinçsiz
682 self-conscious.......................... utangaç/sıkılgan

Notes

Notes